D0578165

GOOD • OLD • DAYS®

DEAR OLD GOLDEN SCHOOL DAYS™

Edited by Ken and Janice Tate

Dear Old Golden School Days™

Editors: Ken and Janice Tate
Managing Editor: Barb Sprunger
Editorial Assistant: Joanne Neuenschwander
Copy Supervisor: Michelle Beck
Copy Editors: Läna Schurb, Judy Weatherford

Publishing Services Director: Brenda Gallmeyer
Art Director: Brad Snow
Assistant Art Director: Nick Pierce
Graphic Arts Supervisor: Ronda Bechinski
Production Artists: Erin Augsburger, Janice Tate
Production Assistants: Marj Morgan, Jessica Tate
Photography: Tammy Christian, Don Clark, Matthew Owen, Jackie Schaffel
Photo Stylists: Tammy Nussbaum, Tammy M. Smith

Chief Executive Officer: David McKee
Book Marketing Director: Dwight Seward

Printed in China
First Printing: 2007
Library of Congress Number: 2006926172
ISBN: 978-1-59217-139-2
Good Old Days Customer Service: (800) 829-5865

Except where noted, all illustrations are courtesy the House of White Birches nostalgia archives.

Photographs on page 87 by and courtesy of Janice Tate.

We would like to thank the following for the art prints used in this book.
For fine-art prints and more information on the artists featured in *Dear Old Golden School Days* contact:
Curtis Publishing, Indianapolis, IN 46202, (317) 633-2070, All rights reserved. www.curtispublishing.com
Norman Rockwell Family Trust, Antrim, NH 03440, (603) 588-3512
Christine Twomey, Lambertville, NJ 08530, (609) 397-0781, www.christinetwomey.artspan.com

1 2 3 4 5 6 7 8 9

Dear Friends of the Good Old Days,

School days, school days,
Dear old golden rule days,
Reading and writing and 'rithmetic,
Taught to the tune of a hickory stick!
You were my queen in calico,
I was your bashful, barefoot beau.
You wrote on my slate, "I love you, Joe,"
When we were a couple of kids.

The words to the chorus of the old song, "School Days," still echo in my mind after all these years. Why is it that our school days mingle bitter and sweet for the remainder of our lives?

Like most of you, some of my fondest memories of childhood revolve around the years I spent in school.

My dear old golden school days were spent in little country schoolhouses in Southwest Missouri. There I picked up the Three R's—and a whole lot more.

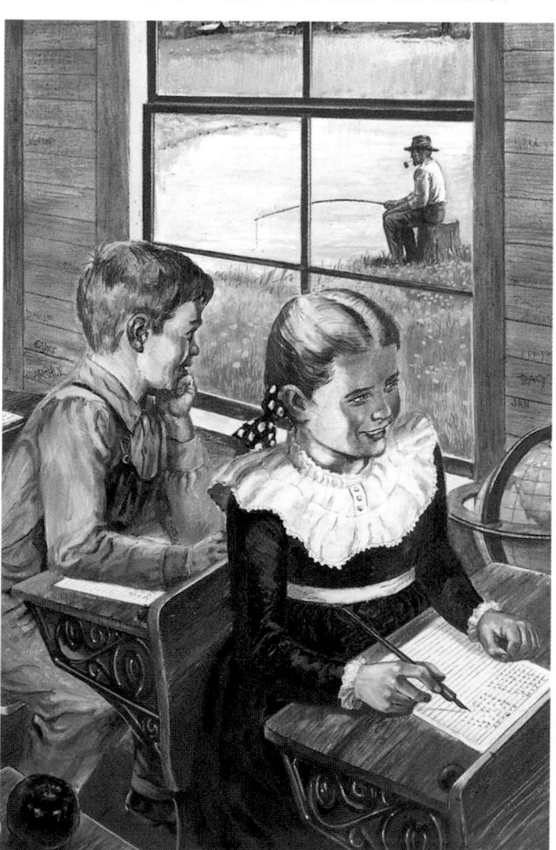

I learned about endurance. Those wooden desk seats sure got hard by the end of a day of torturous attention to educational details. And it didn't help if the day was warm and the fish were biting at the creek not far from school.

I learned about love. Wilma was my first school-days crush. She was from the small community just down the road from our farm. In the second grade I endured other boys' hoots of derision, and gave Wilma a couple of Mama's fresh oatmeal cookies. We ate them at lunch with a glass of milk on the steps of the little stone schoolhouse.

I learned you had to keep your feet in your shoes, even on late summer days when your toes were so hot you thought they would burst into flames—and on warm spring days when fresh green grass beckoned bare feet.

And, there was so much more.

I learned about hard work by helping Teacher with schoolhouse chores like cleaning the blackboard and carrying water.

I learned about patriotism and love of country by reciting the Pledge of Allegiance each morning.

I learned about faith, hope and charity through morning devotionals before school prayer was declared to be unconstitutional.

I guess I learned pretty much everything I needed—and all of that without the aid of television, computers and the rest of education's modern trappings.

I hope you enjoy this collection of true stories from the Good Old Days. They will help you return to your childhood and remember the best years of your life—those dear old golden school days.

Sincerely,

Ken Tate

Contents

SCHOOL
SLOW

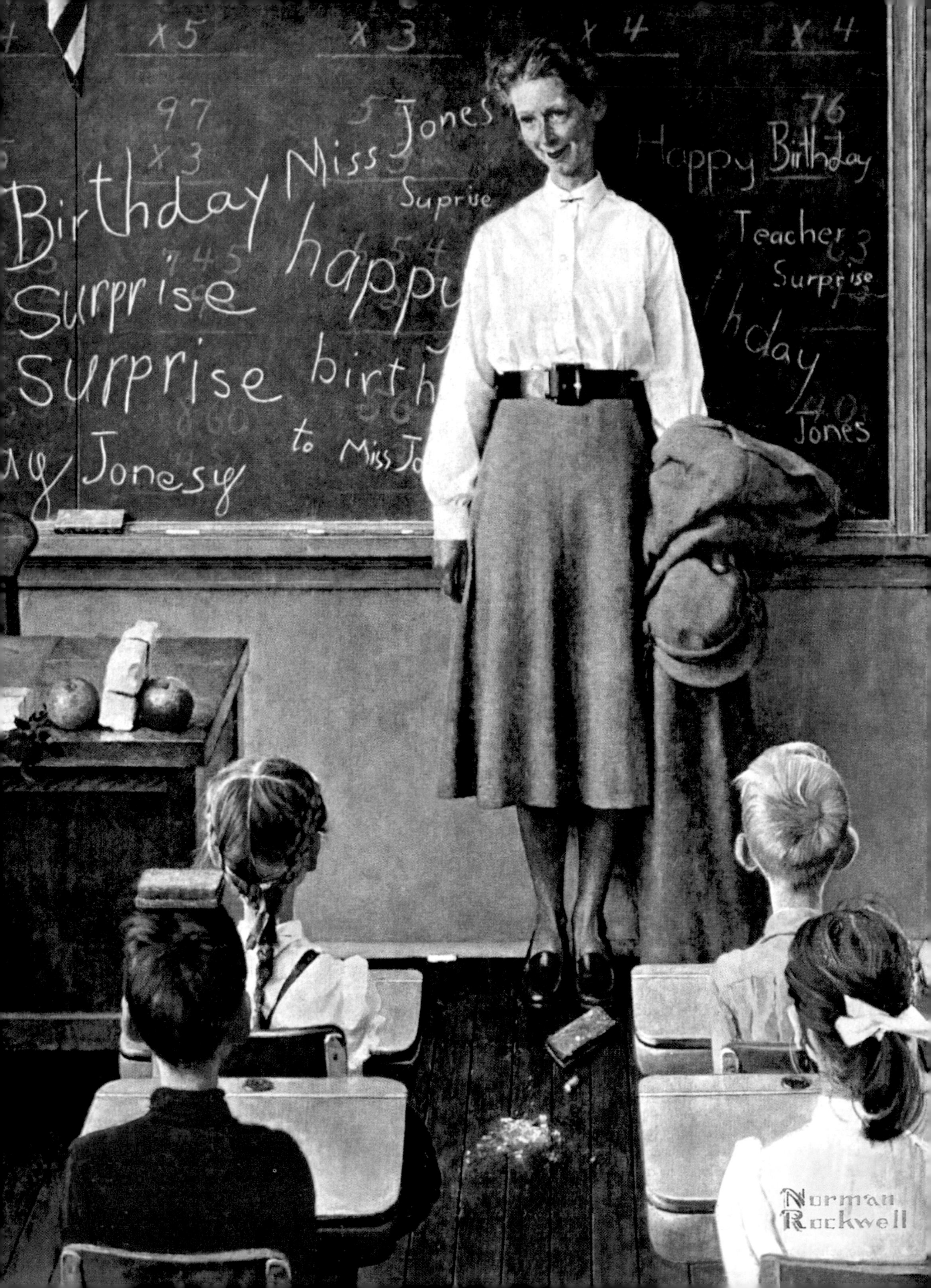
x 5
x 3
x 4
x 4
97
x 3
Jones
76
Miss
Happy Birthday
Birthday
Suprise
Teacher
happy
Surprise
surprise
Surprise
hday
birth
to Miss Jo
Jones
Jonesy
Norman Rockwell

Getting to Know You

Chapter One

Miss Jones came to my rescue, and for that I will forever be in her debt. You see, back in my primary school days in southern Missouri, there was still a decided discrimination against left-handers, and I was about as southpawed as you could get.

My mother's brother, my Uncle Bob, was the only left-handed person in my huge extended family, and he had been switched to being right-handed by coertion from family and educators alike.

Mama remembered that well, so when I showed favoritism to the use of my left hand, she didn't try to change me. Still, being the only left-handed youngster made my early attempts at writing an exercise in hieroglyphics rather than penmanship.

To begin with, our desks in those days were made for right-handed students. There was a nice arm rest for the right forearm and plenty of room for paper to be properly positioned for the vast majority of students who used their right hand.

It was no wonder I learned to write with my left hand curled over the top of my paper. Sure, everyone made fun of the way I did it, but how could I get paper, pencil, hand and arm in position without becoming a contortionist?

And it didn't stop with writing. Scissors were designed for right-handed cutters. I didn't have my own baseball glove, and neither did anyone else. There was a bat, but who could teach a left-handed kid how to swing? If I had been paid a nickel for every time someone told me that something I did looked awkward to them, I certainly would have been a very rich young man.

The whole process frustrated me. I don't know how many times I sang that little schoolyard ditty to myself: "Nobody likes me, everybody hates me. I think I'll go eat worms!"

Miss Jones succeeded in lifting my writing to the brink of legibility.

Then along came Miss Jones and second grade. She wasn't left-handed, but she must have had a left-handed child or something because she was able to help me when no others could. She was endowed with the patience of Job, even though I'm sure I tested it to the limits of endurance. But by the time I finished second grade with her, Miss Jones had succeeded in lifting my writing to the brink of legibility.

More importantly, however, she helped me become more confident and self-assured. She took the time to get to know me. She encouraged me to not treat my left-handedness as some kind of handicap.

"You're special!" she assured me. "I wish *I* were left-handed!"

Looking back, I don't know whether or not that exclamation was true. But it sure meant a lot to a seven-year-old.

The stories in this chapter are dedicated to all of those teachers who took the time to get to know us. We loved them, hated them, feared them and idolized them. Where would we have been without the teachers who so carefully took us under their wings back in the Good Old Days?

—Ken Tate

Hughes

Miss Bloomquist, I Love You

By Nancy Sweetland

She was a marvel. Even now, nearly 60 years later, her face is as clear to me as though she's handing me an assignment. Miss Bloomquist wasn't pretty or stylish. She wore simple dresses or skirts and sweaters. A large but not fat Swedish woman with permed hair, somewhere between 35–45, she was given to serious appraisals and a love of teaching that pulled me through all eight grades in the Minnesota one-room school known only as District 42.

I was 5. I couldn't wait to go to school, but when I finally got there, I was scared of everything. The smells of chalk dust and wood-shaving floor cleaner were overpowering; even today, a whiff of either one takes me right back to my first day of school. The room looked enormous, the desks were way too large, and the big boys in the back seats were scary.

The room looked enormous, and the big boys in the back seats were scary.

But then my mother pushed me unceremoniously at Miss Bloomquist, who had the most beautiful smile I'd ever seen. When she said, "I've been waiting for you," I knew everything was going to be all right.

District 42 was set on a small rise in the middle of southern Minnesota cornfields. It was a white clapboard building about 25 by 40 feet. The big brass bell in the tower didn't ring because the bell rope was missing. There was one door in front and three large windows on each side that were cleaned once each fall by the children's mothers.

During the 1940s all country schoolteachers were probably jacks-of-all-trades, but whatever she was paid, it couldn't have been enough. She was teacher, counselor, mediator, coach and janitor.

Miss Bloomquist drove six miles to school from town every day in an aging Chevrolet, and in the cold months she arrived early enough to have the building heated for us by 9 o'clock. Only a fierce blizzard kept her home; unless she called before 7, we knew she'd be waiting for us, and there were few days we closed early because of weather.

The school's old furnace sprouted vents like octopus tentacles and devoured coal regularly during the winter months. When we began to rub our fingers to keep warm, Miss Bloomquist went to the basement to shovel coal into the furnace. Then the iron door would clang and she would reappear, not a hair out of place. And somehow she always seemed to know if anyone had acted up while she was gone.

We had no running water, just a rusty pump behind the school. Every morning two of the older children had to fill the water container that teetered on a plywood shelf in one corner at the front of the room. If that chore wasn't completed before school time, those kids had to answer to Miss Bloomquist.

Miss Bloomquist had no discipline problems. In spite of handling children of all ages in eight grades—our head count ran from about 15–25, depending on who had moved in or out of the district during the year—I don't remember her ever raising her voice. I believe there was no reason for her to do so. Though the eighth-grade boys were as tall as she was and were sometimes heavier, there was never any question. She was in charge, and we all knew it.

Our desks stood in four rows, with the smaller children in front. The class that was next in session moved to the lesson table near the blackboard. Their studies were recited there and their assignments given out before they were sent back to their desks to work while the next class met. I loved listening to the older classes—by the time I reached those grades, I'd already assimilated a lot of their class work. School was easy; all you had to do was "pay attention."

Miss Bloomquist wasn't all stern you-learn-or-else. Her blue eyes twinkled as she joined us on the playground for ballgames in fall and spring (though she wasn't much of a hitter—or a runner, either, for that matter) and for Fox-and-Geese and snowball fights in the winter. She was our cheerleader and referee, and anyone who didn't play by the rules ended up sitting on the sidelines, wishing they had behaved better.

We had a full hour for eating and playtime, which left us hot and sweaty and far from ready to settle down to learning. So every day after lunch, we put our heads down on our desks while she read aloud a chapter from some ongoing adventure like *Robinson Crusoe* or *Black Beauty.* Someone always pleaded, "Oh, don't stop now," but she held fast and instilled in us the love of story.

There was always something new to keep us interested. When she decided that we needed indoor exercise in inclement weather, she scrounged a couple of mattresses and we learned simple gymnastics on the basement floor. We held jump-rope competitions, played hopscotch on the cement walk, and played Ante-I-Over from one side of the outhouses to the other.

I don't remember any overt lessons on hygiene, but no one was allowed to have lunch without washing hands. This process was accomplished in the basement. A designated "pourer" stood on one side of a basin with a pitcher of water and dribbled it over our soaped hands as, one by one, from smallest to largest, we lined up to wash. Miss Bloomquist stood on the other side of the basin and handed each of us a paper towel for drying. We were expected to say "Thank you."

"Hot lunch" was another of her innovations. She instructed mothers to provide a half-pint jar of soup or hot dish for each child. Then she requisitioned a two-burner hot plate. She set the jars, their lids loosened, in a large pan of water and warmed them over the hot plate all morning in the corner of the little cloakroom. By lunchtime we had hot food to eat with our sandwiches and fruit.

Miss Bloomquist was a firm proponent of encouraging students to realize their potential. I was alone in third grade and tore through the year's work before Christmas, so she moved me up to fourth grade, and I finished that year's work before school let out in the spring. We never had homework; there was always time during school to finish our lessons for the next day if we "paid attention."

There was no running water, no bathroom. There were two two-holer outhouses. Come winter, nobody went to the bathroom without good reason.

Every two weeks, Miss Bloomquist hauled a heavy box of books from the town library. Those of us who had finished our work were privileged to "go to the library," a two-shelved corner in the back of the room. She brought a variety that could please almost everyone, though the boys didn't make as much use of it as the girls did. If we signed a book out, we could take it home overnight. What a treat!

Every Friday after the last period was "industrial arts." We could work on anything we wanted if it was creative and didn't cost much. I don't believe she had a budget for frills. And if what we produced was deemed

Primary school students study a reading assignment. Photo courtesy Janice Tate.

really good, it went up on the wall or on top of the old piano until it was replaced by something better. Once I drew and colored a castle (roughly like Disneyland's castle) that stayed up almost all year. I was so proud!

After Thanksgiving, that last hour was set aside to practice for the annual Christmas program, an astounding (we thought) two-hour performance. Every child would perform in at least one play and recite a poem or "piece" all alone. We could hardly stand ourselves, it was so exciting. I would even get to wear Shirley Temple ringlets curled on rags instead of my usual braids.

The school board, farmers from the district, came a couple of weeks before Christmas and assembled the stage of planks over cement blocks. Then, scattering mothballs, they hung the heavy, old, velvet drapes from a wooden pole suspended from the ceiling. An eighth-grader was named announcer, a much-coveted role deserving of a new dress and curled hair for a girl, or at least a new shirt and necktie for a boy.

Miss Bloomquist saw that every child made a present for his or her parents. My mother still had a box of them when she died—handprints in plaster, childish drawings and clay models.

How did Miss Bloomquist do it all? How did she keep her sanity and turn out children who could read and write better than their city-schooled counterparts? I don't know. But I do know that the lessons I learned in District 42 weren't just lessons in learning. They were lessons in living, in getting along with children of all ages, in never saying, "I can't," and reaching as far as I could to do my best.

Miss Bloomquist was my advisor, my mentor and my friend. She was a marvel.

And, wherever you are, Miss Bloomquist, I love you. ❖

DISTRICT NO. 3
Good Morning,
Children!
Stevan Dohanos

My First Love

By Arthur Jackson

World War II was drawing to a close. I was living with my family in Jamaica, N.Y., a suburban town in Queens County, east of Manhattan. I attended P.S. 109, which was actually in Queen's Village, another 30 miles east of Jamaica. It was a good school for me, one that offered more services than were available in schools closer to my home.

I boarded the bus at 8 o'clock in the morning, changed buses at Hillside Avenue, and arrived at school about 15 minutes before 9. After attending various classes, I spent most of the remainder of the day in homeroom, preparing for the next day's assignments.

P.S. 109 was a three-story brick building, located in a residential area. It was a good place to learn. The students there behaved much better than many of the students did in the inner-city schools. The kids were friendly, and I found them to be delightful companions during my long commute each morning.

I would stand transfixed until her car had passed out of sight.

Then one day I discovered another source of delight. One of my teachers began to awaken a special interest. She had been there every day, but at first I'd taken no special notice of her. Now, all that began to change.

She was a polite person, with short black hair and a quiet demeanor. She wore subdued colors and very ordinary dresses, but they seemed to take on a certain magical quality when she wore them. When she talked, her eyelashes seemed to express what she was saying, and her eyes flashed with enthusiasm.

She drove a green Studebaker, which seemed to be the perfect car for her. During lunch hour in the cafeteria, my eyes were constantly drawn to her.

Miss Willis was a quiet person. She rarely raised her voice, even in the classroom. When she spoke to her classes, her voice was kind, yet serious. I heard total sincerity in her voice. I loved her voice. It was music to my heart.

I would often see her getting into her Studebaker while I was waiting at my bus stop after school. I would stand transfixed until her car had passed out of sight. And when that little green car disappeared, my world was suddenly darker and colder, and I felt sad.

Sometimes when I was at home, I would spend time lounging on the front steps, thinking about Miss Willis, wondering where she lived and how she spent her time after school. I don't think my mother liked to see me sitting idle for too long. Soon her voice would call, "Arthur, I need you to go to the store for milk."

I'd wait as long as possible before responding, but my procrastination time was usually short. I would rise up, do her bidding, and then hurry up to my third-floor bedroom. There, I could hold a book in my hands and pretend to be studying while I continued to daydream about Miss Willis.

On school days, I looked forward to the hour I spent in her classroom, listening to the gentle tones of the voice of my dreams.

When she called on me to recite, I would stretch myself as tall as I could and give her whatever answer she wanted.

In fact, whatever I did, from the Pledge of Allegiance on through the long school day, I did it as perfectly as I could, hoping with all my heart that she would notice me and would realize that everything I did, I did for her.

One afternoon as I headed for the bus stop, I saw Miss Willis driving off. That day her car was spattered with mud. I wished I could have polished up her car for her, but she vanished around a corner in her bedraggled little car.

One day as I was strolling through our neighborhood, I noticed the little green Studebaker parked in a driveway. And, miracle of miracles, there was the light of my life, cutting flowers in the front yard. I stood right across the street from her, and I waved and I waved. But since her back was toward me, she didn't even notice that I was there.

I wondered for a long time what I should do next. I could cross the street and actually talk to her, but I couldn't think of anything meaningful to say, so eventually, I moved on. But my day was complete; my heart was filled with joy again, all because of Miss Willis.

Halfway through the school year I received my report card. I hardly even noticed my other grades, but there, on the fourth line, was the grade Miss Willis had given me for her class. It was a big, beautiful "B."

I was ecstatic. I was sure that that was a better grade than the other kids had received. I was sure that my efforts were paying off. Surely Miss Willis noticed my extra efforts. And maybe she realized that I was much more important to her than the other kids. I clutched that report card in my shirt pocket all the way home. Miss Willis' approval was tucked into the pocket right over my heart. I felt that I had received a national award, and I made sure that Mother noticed that grade I had received from Miss Willis.

One day in spring, I was strolling past Miss Willis' house as I often did after I discovered that she lived right there in the neighborhood. The little green car sat forlornly in the driveway. There was a huge, ugly dent in the front door on the driver's side.

I was furious. She could have been killed in a crash like that! I wondered how she had survived such an attack. If I had known who was responsible, I certainly would have avenged this monstrous attack on the teacher I loved.

As we drew close to the end of the schoolyear, Miss Willis did not come to class for several days. I worried a lot and managed to walk past her house at least once every day, but I saw nothing.

Then, after about a week, she was back in school, looking even more lovely than usual. When I handed her my written work at the end of class, my eyes fell on something I had never seen before, and it brought a cold chill to my heart. There was a new diamond ring on the third finger of her left hand.

I walked down the corrider feeling the darkest despair of my young life. No one could love her as I did. And I couldn't understand how she could find anyone else as important to her as I thought I was. It was all a bittersweet mystery to me. But I knew someone else had taken my place, and I had lost my first love. ❖

A Different Miss Hall

By Don E. Perkins

Probably we've all known a teacher who is such a strict disciplinarian that we assume he or she is totally without compassion. At our grade school, Miss Hall was that teacher. But one day I was surprised to see her tender, caring side when my friend fell off the climbing bars and broke his arm.

Miss Hall, our fourth-grade music teacher, was a large woman. She wasn't fat, just tall, large-boned and very muscular. She looked like the woman shot-putter I saw pictured on the sports page in the newspaper. One look at Miss Hall and you immediately knew she would tolerate no foolishness.

Most of us at Byron Rice Grade School in Des Moines were on our best behavior when we were near her. We didn't want to end up like Frank; she had seen him running in the hallway and promptly grabbed him by the shirt collar. She lifted him off the floor and carried him, dangling and squirming like a freshly caught catfish, down to the front stairway. "Now, young man, I'll give you a chance to do all the running you want to."

Miss Hall released Frank at the foot of the stairs. "You will run up these stairs to the top, stop and turn around, and then walk down. When you reach the bottom, you'll do it all over again." Frank looked down at the floor. His shoulders drooped. "You will do this five times," Miss Hall continued, "and *then* you may come to class."

Nor did we want to have to do what Kendal had had to do. He came to class just two minutes late. When he tried to slip quietly into his seat, Miss Hall blocked him and said, "Young man, next time you either be here on time or don't come at all." Kendal put his hands in front of his face as though he expected Miss Hall to slap him.

"Come with me," she said. "I have a special place for tardy students." She grabbed his elbow and marched him to a corner at the rear of the room. "Now stand there and face the wall."

Miss Hall conducted her classes in the auditorium, where we sat in the first two rows. She stood in front of us or sat at the piano and taught us songs such as *John Peel* and *Green Sleeves.* At Christmas we sang carols, but not modern songs like *Rudolph* or *Frosty the Snowman.* When we reached the upper grades, it was especially thrilling to hear our class sing in two-part harmony.

During recess and over lunch hour, the school playground was alive with youthful exuberance. One morning, Dick Schultz fell off the climbing bars. He screamed and cried as he lay on the ground. Both bones in his forearm were broken just above his wrist and his left hand hung limply.

Miss Hall picked Dick up and cradled him in her strong arms.

I looked toward the building and saw Miss Hall racing toward us. She looked unusually grim. *Oh, Dick's going to get it now,* I thought. *Surely she will scold him for being so clumsy.*

But I was wrong. Miss Hall picked Dick up and cradled him in her strong arms. She spoke softly and reassured him. She wiped the tears and dirt off his face, and then gently carried him into the building for first aid.

Dick was back in school the next day with his left arm in a plaster cast supported by a sling. Most of us crowded around to get a good look at it and to touch it if we could. I think he liked all the attention the cast earned him.

Miss Hall continued to conduct her classes in the same no-nonsense manner, but now I saw her differently. I knew that beneath her tough appearance and hard-boiled manner there lived a caring and compassionate person. I thought, *If I ever fall and break an arm, I hope it's Miss Hall who comes to pick me up.* ❖

Dear Teacher

By Bob Griggs

It was 1936, and I was going to be in the first grade. I didn't quite know what to think about this brand-new thing called school. It was in a big, red brick building, about 10 blocks from our house in Eugene, Ore., and I knew that you went there to learn to read. Heck, that was no big deal; I already knew how to do that pretty good.

I knew that there were people there called "teachers," but that wasn't anything. My parents had been teachers, and I was pretty sure that I didn't want to spend all day with people like them—not when you're 6 years old and grown-up.

Jimmy, who lived next-door, and I had to go by ourselves that first day; our mothers were too busy with our little brothers and sisters. We trudged down the sidewalk, a tall, thin, gangly towhead (me) and a short, stocky, slightly bowlegged Jimmy—two bran'-new students on our first big solo adventure.

"My sister says our teacher is a monster," said Jimmy, gloomily. His sister was in the third grade. "She says that she's got false teeth and hair grows out of her nose. She says that she wears a red wig and carries a whip." I was scared! What do you do when a red-haired monster snaps her whip at you? Fortunately, I never had to find out.

What do you do when a red-haired monster snaps her whip at you?

Mrs. Jackson was tall, slim, dark-haired and quite old—at least 30. She greeted her new charges, found out our names and got us seated. I fell in love with her immediately.

My parents' advice had consisted mostly of "Be good and do what the teacher tells you!" That wasn't much to go on, but I was determined to try my best for this nice lady. The only thing was, Mrs. Jackson didn't tell us what to do! Instead, she started out by reading to us. I can't remember what the story was, but I know it was a whole lot more interesting than the "See Dick run" stuff we got later in our readers.

Mrs. Jackson's desk was at the front of the room, and we quickly discovered that she almost never used it except to hold some papers and books. She moved around all the time, walking up and down the aisles when she read aloud to us. I began to feel that she was speaking just to me, and when she'd look up and catch my rapt gaze, she'd smile, and I felt warm and special. When I was reading out loud myself, she would stand beside me and put her arm around me, and I felt so smart and able to do anything she asked.

Strangely enough, when she treated the other kids the same way, I didn't feel the least bit jealous. She had plenty of love for all of us.

In art, everyone in the class did the most marvelous drawings. Mrs. Jackson told us so. It didn't matter if one's chimney leaned sideways or the grass smeared or there were too many fingers on people's hands. Mrs. Jackson loved them all. She even encouraged us to bring drawings we did at home. Every bit of wall space was covered with them, including many of mine.

I remember one wonderful week when she asked everyone to bring a pinewood orange crate to school. We were mystified, as were our parents—and every grocery store in the area—but we lugged them in. Mrs. Jackson had arranged for space and help from the school janitor, and under their supervision, we learned to hammer and saw and paint—boys and girls alike. We made those crates into chairs and tables and bookcases—all of them painted bright red. We used them in the classroom and got to take them home at the end of the year.

I didn't know if there was a Mr. Jackson, so I asked my parents. They told me that Mr. Jackson had been a policeman and was killed when a bad man shot at his motorcycle.

He and Mrs. Jackson had been married for just a little while, and they didn't have any children. I remember feeling so bad about that, but I think that I understood a little, even then, that we were *all* Mrs. Jackson's children. She loved us indiscriminately, encouraged us, looked after us, cared about us and taught us.

I wonder how many hundreds of little ones she lavished her talents on over the years. How many of us got our first joyous experiences in reading, writing, and just plain learning from this very special woman!

At the end of my first school year, my family moved to the country. I never saw Mrs. Jackson again. I had many teachers over the years—some good, some wonderful, and a few a little like Jimmy's sister's monster with the whip. I realize now that all of them were measured against Mrs. Jackson. I wish that I could tell her.

Still, I guess I can in a way, for nearly 70 years later, a small person inside of me can still feel her arm across his shoulders and hear her warm voice whispering, "Go ahead, Bobby, I *know* you can do it."

Thank you, Mrs. Jackson. I love you. ❖

The Paddling That Backfired!

By Bettie Vance Steelman

My dad was reared in a small coal-mining town in southern West Virginia. In 1932, as a lad of 8, my dad would meet a couple of his friends at the company store where they would chat awhile before walking on to school. One morning, one of his buddies offered him a box of matches.

The matches manufactured at that time were very flammable and would strike anywhere. He tried to place the box of matches in one of his front pockets, but he had forgotten that both were filled with marbles. He stuck the box in his back pocket, but they felt too bulky. So he took the matches out of the box and stuck them, loose, in his pocket. Then he and his buddies proceeded on to school.

Soon after their arrival, class began. A short time later, he began talking to his friend. The teacher stopped and said, "Theon, be quiet, please." He stopped talking, but after a few moments, he remembered something else he needed to tell his friend. As soon as the teacher heard my dad whispering again, she said, "Theon, come up here."

As he reluctantly approached her desk, she got out her paddle and said, "Put both hands on the desk and bend over." He meekly followed her instructions.

The normal punishment was five licks. But after two licks, the teacher stopped. Wondering what was going on, he slowly turned his head. Through a cloud of billowing smoke, he saw his teacher's pale, shocked face. She seemed to be on the verge of fainting.

The paddle had easily ignited the forgotten matches in my dad's back pocket.

He pulled up the teacher's chair for her to sit in. From that day forward, she always sent disobedient students to the principal's office for their paddling. ❖

Lessons Well Learned

By Lois O. Bruce

Playing the piano was a dream of mine for years when I was a young girl living in the sandhills of western Nebraska. But my growing-up years coincided with the 1930s Depression, and few families had the money for a piano or piano lessons. Mine certainly didn't. So, when my eighth-grade teacher, Mr. Fitzgerald, told our class that if any of us wanted to stay in at recess, he would teach us the basic steps of one-fingered piano playing on the school piano, I was first in line. At the time, I didn't realize how those well-learned lessons taken in the Good Old Days would pay off in the distant days to come.

If you were lucky, you had at least one outstanding teacher like Mr. Fitzgerald. Of course, we thought he was too into math (fractions, multiplication tables and decimals). He also emphasized correct grammar and parts of speech, and—too often for us—he announced the dreaded assignment, "Today we will diagram sentences."

There were no social studies then. We studied geography (there were fewer countries in the world then) and history (all those dates and battles). Spelling bees were weekly events between opposing class teams. Reading was so important that every student had to have a library card at the local library and be able to report on a book a month to show that we had used it.

Mr. Fitzgerald also read aloud to us—yes, to eighth-graders! He read *Kidnapped* and King Arthur stories, and poetry, a lot of which we had to memorize.

I still remember *Snowbound* by John Greenleaf Whittier. As Mr. Fitzgerald read it to us, snow was swirling outside the classroom windows, making the poem come to life.

There was no P.E. back then, but we had to turn out for two recesses a day. Mr. Fitzgerald organized ballgames and a game we could only play when there was snow on the ground called Fox-and-Goose. There was plenty of snow in winter in the sandhills—so much that we were heartily tired of that game by spring.

We also had what are now called "extracurricular activities." We called them fun! We had art lessons in which we learned to use perspective in drawing the scenery around us and use colors in pleasing

I am in the front desk, second row, on the right. Mr. Fitzgerald, the music teacher, is at the rear, standing behind his desk.

combinations. We had music—singing sessions during which we sang from the *True Blue Songbook*. I remember *Flow Gently, Sweet Afton*, *Camptown Races* and *Row, Row, Row Your Boat,* during which the boys amused themselves by getting the girls all off kilter!

And we started a school newspaper, learning to write factual aritcles as well as fictional serials and editorials.

But those recesses were my favorite times at school because I was having piano lessons! Before we could touch the keys, we had to learn to read the names of the notes on the scale. Mr. Fitzgerald did that in the time-honored way by using the sentence "Every Good Boy Does Fine," in which the first letter of each word was the name of a line on the scale from the bottom to the top. And the word "FACE" named the spaces in between.

When we could tell him the name of every note in a piece of music, he showed us middle C and the progressive notes on the keyboard. Then he turned us loose to pick, one-fingered, the melodies that were sharpless and flatless.

Later, we could add one sharp or flat piece to our repertoire. We were soon able to play one-fingered—but recognizable—tunes during those special recesses. As with all our lessons—math, grammar or music—no new phase was introduced until we had thoroughly learned the previous lesson.

I came to value this "learn it well" philosophy many years later after I was married and had a daughter. In the intervening years I had done nothing with the piano, but I wanted to be sure that Kathy had lessons, so we bought her a used piano on her sixth birthday. It came with a bench, which held a few pieces of sheet music, one of which was *Silent Night*.

As I looked the music over, the "Every Good Boy Does Fine" and "FACE" lessons came back to me, along with the location of middle C. With one finger, I hesitantly started picking out notes on the keyboard. Very slowly, *Silent Night* became recognizable! We were all amazed, especially when I told them that it was lessons from my days as an eighth-grader that were guiding my fingers on the keys. (I had been an eighth-grader in 1938—and this was in 1968!

Yes, in the Good Old Days, schools and teachers taught us lessons that we remembered well in the years that followed. ❖

IVANHO
PROBLEMS
Steven Dohanos

Mr. Jones

By Bob Becker

In the book of the Great State Papers of New Jersey, which every student received upon graduation from eighth grade in 1939, I have the autograph of our only male teacher at that time. It is simply signed, “Thomas P. Jones.” Mr. Jones was a manual-training teacher who taught seventh- and eighth-grade students. He was there only one day per week. The other days he taught at the other township schools. What else he spent his time with I have no idea. Regardless, I want to tell you what Mr. Jones meant to me.

He was a thorough teacher in that he demonstrated how something could be made with the use of tools. When I say tools, I mean hand tools. There were no electric tools such as we know them today.

The more he talked, the more I wanted to learn. You could choose a project of your liking, and then he would start you on it. If you came to some part that you didn’t quite understand, he’d be there to guide you through the steps.

When I say tools, I mean hand tools. There were no electric tools.

I only got to complete two projects through seventh and eighth grades because Mr. Jones saw that I learned quickly and gave me other jobs to do, sometimes even helping other students who were a bit slower catching on.

But what I learned over and above that was something I carried away with me, and over the following years, I have used that knowledge in my work and especially during the 40-some years that I was in my own shop business.

Most of the students didn’t care anything about using tools and were careless in their use as well. When I went to use a jack plane one day, I found it so dull and full of nicks that I asked Mr. Jones if I could sharpen it. Right then and there he showed me how to do it on the grinder. From then on I sharpened all of the cutting tools: planes, wood chisels and such.

He also showed me how to file and set hand saws: crosscut, rip and backsaws. If it was done correctly, I could take a handsaw, put a pencil line on a board with a square, and either cut right up to the line, leaving a faint pencil mark, or split the line so the teeth of the saw would straddle the line equally.

I learned the name of each tool in the shop and its purpose.

When I built a secretary desk, I started it in seventh grade and finished it in eighth grade. We only had a one-hour class one day a week, and I couldn’t accomplish a lot in so little time. This is where dexterity paid off.

On that particular job, I got to use many of the hand tools, and in so doing, I learned how each was used for a particular job. Making the mortise-and-tenon joints in the legs was the most time-consuming task, but over a couple of one-hour periods, I finished them.

Today a modern carpenter or cabinet maker can make up a mortise-and-tenon joint in a matter of minutes if he knows how. Most carpenters in today's world don't even know what a hand tool is, let alone how to use one.

When I explain to people who have seen my desk that it was made by a 13-year-old boy using only hand tools, they find it hard to believe. After 67 years, my desk is still as tight in the joints as it was when I finished it. Mr. Jones taught me that a job worth doing is a job worth doing well, and a good job speaks for itself but a poor job isn't worth speaking about. I have never forgotten that advice.

Mr. Jones has been gone for a very long time now. Wherever he may be, I hope that he's still teaching young boys the value of doing good work with their hands and heart, just as he taught me back in the Good Old Days. ❖

I built this secretary desk (below) under Mr. Jones' guidance during seventh and eighth grades. It's still as sturdy today as it was when I built it.

The Willow Cat

By Margaret Widdemer

They call them "pussy willows,"
But there's not a cat to see,
Except the little furry toes
That stick out on the tree.

I think that very long ago
When I was just born new,
There must have been whole pussy cats
Where just their toes stick through.

And every spring it worries me;
I cannot ever find
Those willow cats that ran away
And left their toes behind!

I am an 80-year-old retired schoolteacher. I taught for 32 years in elementary school. Every year when a student would bring in the first pussy willows, I would recite this poem and then have them learn it.

—*Submitted by Hazel Kennison, Elmwood Park, N.J.*

The Christmas Spirit

By Audrey Corn

Christmas in the 1940s was special. As my sister and I counted down the December days and the excitement mounted, our elders expressed deepening concern. Jennie and I needed to focus more on "the true spirit of Christmas," they chided.

The grown-ups explained that Christmas was about love and caring. About peace. And goodwill. They reminded us that we were celebrating the birth of our Savior. I meant no disrespect to the Baby Jesus, but it was so easy to get caught up in the holiday hoopla. The gifts! The tree! The school pageant!

Fortunately, my seventh-grade teacher recognized that the best way for us to experience the true spirit of Christmas was to live it, not hear lectures about it.

To this end, Miss Braxton shared with us a packet of letters addressed to Santa Claus. They'd come, she explained, from a friend who taught first grade in one of the city's poorer neighborhoods.

"My friend doesn't have enough volunteers to answer these letters, so I told her we'd help out," Miss Braxton said.

"I'm going to set one rule," Miss Braxton continued. "You can't spend money on this project." Miss Braxton's rule wouldn't get any argument from us!

My classmates and I were better off than the youngsters who wrote those letters, but back in the 1940s in Brooklyn, N.Y., nobody had money for much beyond the necessities. Miss Braxton passed the letters around the classroom so we'd all have a chance to read them. Most of the children asked for toys. Some letters were funny. A few were sad.

One youngster knew that Santa had to bring a food basket because his parents couldn't afford Christmas dinner. But if Santa had an extra toy lying around the workshop, could he please, please bring that, too!

Two boys in my class volunteered to answer this letter. With help from their dads, they fashioned a sturdy wagon using orange crates and a set of wheels from a discarded baby carriage.

My own contribution was the Betsy doll I had received when I was little. With assistance from my dear mama, I outfitted my Betsy in a new dress and ruffled bonnet.

Of course, there were some requests that we couldn't fill. A first-grader wanted Santa to help his sister recover from that dreaded scourge of the 1940s—polio.

"My sister can't run or play. She can't do anything except lie in her iron lung. Please make her well, Santa," the little boy wrote.

Miss Braxton and our class discussed the problem at length. Sadly, we had no cure for polio. Eventually, Terence Neely came up with a good idea. Terence contributed a freshly painted white gramophone that his parents had given to him when he was 5.

The rest of us searched through our closets, basements and attics. The result was an impressive collection of phonograph records. The little boy's sister still couldn't run or jump or play, but now she'd be able to wile the hours away listening to her new Victrola.

Slowly but surely, we responded to all the letters. Miss Braxton rewarded each of us with an A in Social Studies. But our real reward had nothing to do with A's, B's or C's. Our gift was knowing that on Christmas morning, Santa wouldn't disappoint those small children.

While other grown-ups lectured us about love and goodwill, our seventh-grade teacher taught by example. She proved that we are never too old or too young, too rich or too poor, to give of ourselves. From Miss Braxton we learned what our elders meant when they spoke of the "true spirit of Christmas" back in the Good Old Days. ❖

She Made Footprints

By Lee Hill-Nelson

My sisters and I sat on our front porch, eating after-school snacks. In the far distance, a familiar figure dressed in white trudged down the dusty road leading from the schoolhouse. We wondered who Mrs. Molly Reece, my fourth-grade teacher, would visit today.

Mrs. Reece taught third, fourth and fifth grades, all in one room in the Bridle Bit School in the Texas Panhandle. Most any day after school it was not unusual to see her headed toward a student's home for a talk with the parents about a discipline problem, a health problem or whatever needed to be dealt with. What was unusual was that she walked everywhere she went. It was 1931 and the Great Depression had begun. She was a widow and had no car.

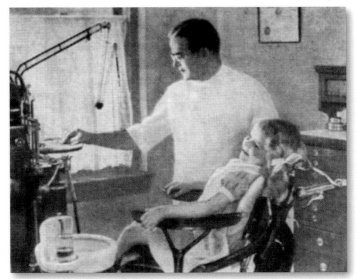

1937 Fletcher's Castoria advertisement, House of White Birches nostalgia archives.

I thought she was 100 years old. Today, I'd guess her to be 60. I see her now—white marcelled hair framing her wrinkled face. Some folks described her as being stout. Others said she was heavy on her feet.

It was a typical West Texas spring day, warm and sunny, a bit of dust blowing, with whirlwinds popping up here and yonder. As she rounded the last bend in the road, I saw that she was coming to our house. *Did I do something wrong at school?* I wondered.

She climbed the wooden steps to our porch, short of breath and perspiring. Her hand touched my shoulder and she said, "It's going to be all right. May I speak to your father?"

Papa looked surprised when he saw her on the porch. She stood there smiling a sweet smile, looking up at this tall, handsome, dark-skinned man, daring to confront him, something I was afraid to do.

A decayed tooth with an abscess on my gum caused me pain at school. Mrs. Reece did not like that. Despite my awakening at night and Mama "doctoring" it with cloves and heating a washcloth over a kerosene lamp to place on my jaw, Papa would not relent and take me to the dentist because he said, "It would be a waste of money."

Papa was one of three trustees for the school district and had a vote as to which teachers to hire. I wondered how Mrs. Reece could be so brave. She dared to risk her job. In her quiet manner, she told Papa that the toothaches interrupted my schoolwork; that taking care of teeth when children are young is very important.

At first, Papa seemed angry. But whether from embarrassment or from her gentle persuasion, Papa gradually relaxed and promised to take me to the dentist on the coming Saturday.

Mrs. Reece stayed awhile for a chat before she said goodbye to us and headed toward the setting sun. Her day's work was done, her mission accomplished.

She was more than a teacher. She made footprints on the dusty roads she walked. She made footprints on her students' lives. She taught reading, writing and arithmetic—and she taught us the importance of caring. ❖

Worth Her Weight

By Renie Szilak Burghardt

I started school in my new country, the United States of America, as a displaced person in January 1952. At 15, "displaced" described my legal status and my fragile self-esteem, as well. My grandparents and I had suffered through World War II in our native Hungary, living four years in a refugee camp before coming to America.

So there I was, a mousy, shy girl who spoke with a thick Hungarian accent, and was barely noticed by her beautiful American peers. For beautiful is what they were to me, these girls with their ponytails, bobby socks and carefree, fun-loving ways. I longed to be like them.

The all-girls' school was run by nuns, and girls came from all parts of the city of Cleveland to attend. Many of them drove their own cars to get there. I lived in a rental house near the school, so I walked.

I was quite aware that sending me to a school with tuition was a sacrifice on my grandparents' part. After all, we were newcomers, and extra money was scarce. And I felt lucky to be accepted, since my English was not up to par. A friend hadn't been so lucky; she was put back to the sixth grade, and was so mortified that a year later, she quit school to work in a sewing factory.

By the time June came around, I had been in my new school for five months. I was still shy and mousy and barely noticed by the other girls, but despite my poor academic performance, I passed to the 10th grade! I spent my first summer in America working at a local dime store, and hanging out with friends in ethnic establishments.

Summer ended much too soon, and in September it was time to don the blue-and-gold jumper and white blouse and go back to school. I entered school with dread; although some of the girls greeted me cheerily, I had not changed into a swan over the summer, and I knew it. Then I walked into Sister Mary Ann's sophomore English class, and soon everything changed!

Sister Mary Ann had twinkling blue eyes, a kind face and a gentle, understanding manner. On the first day, she inquired about my life in front of the class so my classmates could better understand why I was "different" from them, she said. I felt as though I had met my guardian angel! Just before class was over, she gave us our first written assignment of the new term.

"I want all of you to write an essay of four or five pages about something momentous in your lives," she said. I wasn't too sure I knew what an essay was, but for the first time since I had come to that school, I put my heart and soul into an assignment. I wrote about what it was like being crammed onto a ship with hundreds of hopeful refugees. I wrote about Dave, my first American friend. I wrote about seeing the Statue of Liberty for the first time. And as I wrote, I realized that I really liked writing.

I wrote about seeing the Statue of Liberty for the first time.

The day after we handed in our essays, Sister Mary Ann asked me to read my essay to the entire class. I began very nervously, but gained confidence as I went on, and when I was finished, my classmates gave me a big hand!

Later, in the hallway, girls who had never spoken to me before came to tell me how much they liked my essay. And even later, when the essay was actually published in a popular magazine of the 1950s called *The American Girl,* I was dubbed a "real writer," and enjoyed it tremendously. But what was most important to me was that my classmates had finally accepted me. I was one of them!

Teachers like Sister Mary Ann, who change their pupils' lives for the better, are worth their weight in gold. And they are never forgotten by their grateful pupils! ❖

EORGE WASHINGTON 173
ABRAHAM LINCOLN 180
Griffiths

Miss Elsie

By Roxie Frans Olmstead

The one thing that brings on nostalgia for me more than anything else is remembering my school days and teachers. It was such a happy time. Elsie L. Higdon came into my life as my third- and fourth-grade teacher at Magna City School, a rural school in Butler County, Kan. In the 1930s, teachers were respectfully called "Miss," "Mrs." or "Mr." plus their surname. But on the very first day of school, Elsie L. Higdon announced that we could call her "Miss Elsie." Perhaps that is why we instantly felt so close to her. "Elsie" seemed so personal, yet "Miss" gave her respect needed by a teacher.

I have learned from old records that Miss Elsie came our way with 10 years of experience and a state life teaching certificate, which earned her $75 per month. She saw to it that we covered all the required material for each grade level.

As was expected, she was a strict disciplinarian. After all, one of a teacher's important duties, then as now, was to keep a roomful of live wires grounded.

The oil boomtown of Magna City, Kan., had built our three-room, two-story brick school building in 1924. By the time Miss Elsie arrived, the boom had ended and the town's population was declining. Only one room of the building was used.

Miss Elsie recognized each pupil's talent and tried to develop it.

The school's 17 pupils included four from my family. One sister graduated the first year Miss Elsie taught at our school. The next year, there were 10 pupils with one attending only part of the year. All the pupils' fathers were oilfield workers except one, and he was a farmer.

There wasn't much rain during the Dirty '30s, but on one rare occasion, water actually ran in a slough not far from school. Miss Elsie took advantage of it by teaching us how to make and sail folded-paper sailboats.

When my sister Dorothy bent over to sail her boat, she saw she had reached across a snake. Dorothy jumped back, ran, and screamed, "Snake!" The older students immediately labeled it a rattlesnake and plotted to kill it, but Miss Elsie said "No." She thought it was a bull snake and explained that they were good snakes and shouldn't be killed.

Children reared in that location learned early on to recognize a rattlesnake. The older pupils disagreed with Miss Elsie about what kind of snake it was. Pupils seldom argued with a teacher in those days, and I was afraid my older sister would get into trouble for arguing, but she was adamant that it was a rattlesnake.

Miss Elsie finally agreed that they could toss one rock at the snake, and if it rattled, she would let them kill it. They threw the rock and the snake immediately coiled and rattled. "Kill it!" Miss Elsie shouted.

The first year Miss Elsie taught our school, she and another teacher from an adjoining district shared a rented house. The second year she asked for and received permission from the school board to live in the school building. She set up living quarters in a small offstage dressing room in the basement where she had a bed, table and chairs, and a kerosene cookstove.

On weekends Miss Elsie went to her parents' home in Potwin, Kan., or visited her brother, Phil Higdon, the county superintendent of schools, in El Dorado, Kan. Both Potwin and El Dorado were in our county.

They threw the rock and the snake immediately coiled and rattled.

It was a lonely life for Miss Elsie in the evenings during the week. She let each girl take a turn spending the night with her. We were excited to have this rare privilege.

Miss Elsie couldn't seem to get enough of us during school. During her second year as our teacher, she actually took six of us girls to her parents' home in Potwin one weekend.

We all lived in small, one-story oilfield houses provided by the oil companies. I viewed Miss Elsie's parents' two-story house as a mansion. I remember my fascination with the dollhouse Mr. Higdon had made for Miss Elsie when she was a child. That weekend was one I'll never forget.

We had free gas in the oilfield, but no electricity. We made toast under the oven broiler in our gas stoves. But that dried the bread out, and it wasn't very tasty. At breakfast at the Hidgons', we quickly consumed all the bread in the house when they toasted it in an electric toaster. Miss Elsie's father went to a grocery store for more bread. It was usually closed on Sundays, but I think the grocer was a friend and opened up just for him.

Miss Elsie had what she called a pajama parade. After we girls had dressed for bed in our pajamas, each of us performed her specialty to entertain our host and hostess. Some sang, some gave readings, and I performed an acrobatic routine I had worked up.

Miss Elsie recognized each pupil's talent and tried to develop it. If someone had a talent for giving readings, you could be sure he gave one at every school program. The same applied to singing. She wanted me to develop my acrobatic skills. She was going to attend summer school at Emporia and tried to get my parents to let me go with her to attend a summer school for children that taught gymnastics as part of the curriculum.

I started school at age 5 and took both first and second grades the first year. My three older sisters often played school, and once they started to school, they would no longer play the role of pupil, but insisted on being a teacher. So I had three teachers as a preschooler. I knew how to read, do simple arithmetic problems and write by the time I started school. I was always two grades ahead of my age.

My parents refused Miss Elsie's offer because they were afraid I'd advance another grade if I went to summer school. That would catch me up with a sister, and they didn't want to discourage her. Although I didn't get to participate in the gymnastics school, I appreciated the fact that Miss Elsie tried.

Miss Elsie also took an interest in community affairs. With my mother she co-hosted a bridal shower for a young woman in the community. This type of participation endeared her to the entire community.

Later Miss Elsie married a grocer in a nearby town and changed her name to Smith. She had one daughter, Karen, who became a minister. Miss Elsie was widowed early when her husband died after a heart attack. My mother heard from her off and on for years. Miss Elsie spent the last years of her life in a nursing home after suffering a stroke.

It pleasures me to ask teachers today if they'd like to take six of their pupils home with them for a weekend, just to hear their comments. Their responses only reinforce my appreciation of Miss Elsie, and I relish telling them about her. ❖

Whistlin' in Dixie

By Dee Dyson

Everything I learned about whistling I learned from Miss Middleton. She taught piano lessons in a rural eastern North Carolina community where I went to school in the 1940s. One Friday a month, our principal asked Miss Middleton to take charge of student assembly. While one of her students pounded out a peppy Sousa march on the yellowed keys of the bulky black upright, we filed in, grade by grade, one through seven, row by row, from front to back of the auditorium.

Then Miss Middleton stepped from stage left, carrying an American flag like a soldier on parade. Instead of the usual opening prayer, she sang in an operatic voice:

"While the storm clouds gather
Far across the sea,
Let us pledge allegiance
To a land that's free."

With a nod to her accompanist and a lift of her right hand, she ordered us: "Sing! Sing! *Sing!* All together now, boys and girls: 'God bless America, land that I love!'" We sang the chorus three times, getting louder each round.

After that, she warmed up for her whistling repertoire. She began with eyes lowered, chin tucked, lips tightly puckered. With an ascending "do-re-mi-fa-so-la-ti-do," she looked toward the ceiling, her neck stretching out like a crowing hen. A descending "do-ti-la-so-fa-mi-re-do" lowered her chin back to normal.

She stood straight, her elongated face creased by her profession, brown hair piled high on her head like a bird's nest. With perfect enunciation, in a musical voice that seemed to slide upward, she asked, "And how are my young warblers today? Have we been practicing our whistling?"

Most of us raised our hands. She tried to teach us bird calls in assembly once, but the boys trilled catcalls and the girls giggled. All that blowing in each other's faces was too much like exchanging germs. (Mama said girls shouldn't whistle because it wrinkled their faces and cracked their lips, but I practiced in front of the mirror anyway.)

Sometimes, leaning to one side and cupping her hand to one ear, she would ask, "Is that a meadowlark I hear?" The flutelike tones that escaped from her compressed lips sounded like they came from a grassy countryside. She followed with the reedy call of the bobolink, starting low and rollicking upward, and ended with the lilting notes of a bobwhite. We always joined in on that one.

But Miss Middleton didn't just imitate bird calls. She interspersed her whistling with songs and expected us to memorize every stanza. Making sweeping motions with both arms and throwing her head back, she directed her motley fledglings, "My country 'tis of thee, sweet land of liberty, let freedom ring." She also whistled and sang the melodies of Stephen Foster.

I marveled at how such pretty music could come from a not-so-pretty face.

But of all her trills, tweets and twitters, my favorite was *Indian Love Call.* When she stood center stage, hands clasped to her bosom, head tilted as if looking toward the mountaintops, there was no doubt the whistler was emulating the longing love song of Jeanette MacDonald. She whistled to "Calling you-oo-oo," and the "Answering you-oo-oo-oo." The high treble notes had the piano player nearly flying from her perch on the bench.

Miss Middleton, that bird of a woman, not only entertained us, but also commanded our attention and connected some of us with our first moments of music appreciation. Many times over the years, when I've listened to someone whistle or I've heard the clear call of the bobwhite, I've thought of her. And when I watch Bacall as she asks Bogey, "You do know how to whistle, don't you?" I say, "No, I never learned, but it wasn't because I didn't hear it from the best." ❖

A Special Teacher

By Dottie Brunt

When our thoughts go back to childhood days, they rest the longest on the time we spent in school. The first seven years of my schooling are forever associated with the one and only teacher I had during that time. She was of medium height and weight, with dark brown hair always in place, dark soft eyes behind rimless glasses, a smile that showed even white teeth, and an air that said we would work together with no nonsense. And if there was, she could deal with that as methodically as she dealt with everything else.

We all were needed to help her run the one-room school. The boys took turns bringing in the slabs of wood to burn in the potbellied stove surrounded by a metal shield. We stood behind it to get warm on cold winter days when we first arrived at school.

Our drinking fountain was a ceramic jug with a spigot that an older student kept filled by hauling water from a farm down the hill. A row of nails above the water cooler held the students' cups.

"A man who wants a garden fair must bend his back and dig!"

The most honored job was running the flag up the pole every morning and taking it down in late afternoon. But it was more of a reward to be chosen to wash the blackboards at the close of school each week. The teacher always swept the floor herself at day's end, and perhaps twice a year she cleaned and oiled it. She must have also washed the window.

One little chore that even a small first-grader could handle was emptying the pencil sharpener. We were only allowed to use it at recess, though, because the noise from the sharpener might interfere with our concentration.

She placed great importance on memorization. I don't mean just dates, places and names from history or multiplication tables. We had to memorize at least one poem a month, always appropriate to the time of year, such as Columbus for October. Others emphasized an ethic, such as: "Be strong! We are not here to dream, to drift; we have hard work to do and loads to lift."

There were sad ones, too, like the one about the Little Toy Dog covered with dust, waiting for a little boy to wake from death and play again. Sometimes we had to repeat a long paragraph from a reading book or recite the Gettysburg Address that we learned about in history class.

I love to remember the words and expressions she used. It was ridiculous to think something was impossible and preposterous if homework was not completed. We would be back to the poetry again:

"A man who wants a garden fair must bend his back and dig!"

She taught us so many things. We had music—not just morning songs, but how to recognize the different symbols, and we learned the scales and note values. We read about the great composers, and if anyone could play piano or sing, she would have them share their talent.

My First School Play by Jay Killian, House of White Birches nostalgia archives

We performed a little drama and put on programs for the public twice a year. One was in the evening in the fall, which we combined with a fund-raiser. After our entertainment of skits, recitations and musical solos, there was a box social with a square dance. The money raised by auctioning off the boxes went toward something the school could use as a little extra treat. One year it was a radio, and on it we heard President Roosevelt declare war on Japan. I remember the teacher looking worried while we quietly listened to the president's words.

This teacher gave us a social life, and that was very important to children living on isolated farms. We exchanged gifts at Christmas. She owned a Santa suit and one of the big boys would don it before he distributed the presents that had been placed under the big, decorated tree. Each holiday was marked with a party or something special to set it apart from the regular school day.

The last-day-of-school hot-dog roast was my favorite. We actually built a fire behind the school and roasted hot dogs on long sharpened sticks. We used money in our little school treasury to buy the buns, mustard and relish. An eighth-grade girl would squeeze lemons for lemonade, and some mothers would donate freezers of ice cream.

After we had stuffed ourselves with all the food and played games and made the schoolroom neat, we said goodbye to each other for that year. I always dissolved in tears when I said goodbye to this teacher who was also a friend and the most important person in my life. I couldn't wait for September to roll around again because I never saw her during the summer.

I remember playing outside at recess time. In winter we would play Fox-and-Geese if there was snow on the ground. In the fall or spring we would play Kick-the-Stick or baseball. I would see her peering out the window to make sure everyone was playing happily and fairly.

She believed in putting order in one's life. We played hard, studied hard and tried to do our best. She had high hopes for us and took pride in each of us.

Years later that little school was closed, and I heard that our teacher had gone to teach in a large city school. I've never pictured her in that setting where she wouldn't have been principal, teacher, nurse, friend, even janitor, all rolled into one.

But I know she had the same dedication that she always showed us. I hope her students appreciated all her fine qualities and learned as much from this devoted lady as I did. She truly was a "born teacher." ❖

The Love of My Life

By Dorothy Rieke

One day when I was 4 years old, I stood looking through the kitchen screen door and declared, "I want to be a teacher when I grow up!" In the years that followed, I never thought of doing anything else. I constantly "played school" with friends, and prepared worksheets and art projects for imaginary students at my little desk.

As a high-school junior I took a year of "normal training." That course and an excellent teacher intensified my desire to teach.

About that time, I also began taking the odious teacher's examinations given by the county superintendent. These tests were comprehensive and difficult, and I had to pass them to qualify for a third-grade elementary certificate.

After graduating from high school at age 16, I entered a nearby college for an intensive, 12-week course designed to prepare me for rural teaching. This course of study was truly an endurance test. It included subjects such as classroom management, music and methods. It all seemed far removed from actual classroom teaching as far as I was concerned, but I persevered.

I moved forward and tried to reason with the crying, red-faced child.

The course on playground supervision was helpful, as the instructor introduced us to children's games that we could teach to our students. We kept carefully documented notebooks so that we could recall those games later.

This course required that we wear slacks. My only pair of slacks was made of wool, but I had no money to buy different ones. So I wore those hot, woolen slacks 45 minutes a day during the hot summer months. They were uncomfortable, to say the least; besides being itchy, the heavy fabric made my lower body feel like it was encased in a steam bath.

In the meantime, I was hired to teach students in a brick schoolhouse three miles from our farm. My mother had taught there before her marriage, and I'm sure her reputation helped me obtain the job.

The school-board members, including two of Mother's former students, promised to have the schoolhouse cleaned before school started. After that, I'd be responsible for keeping the premises clean and tidy.

As soon as possible after summer school, I visited the vacant school. It was surrounded by tall weeds, but I was excited and happy.

It was too good to be true—my own schoolhouse, and soon I'd have pupils to teach! My longtime dreams were becoming reality.

I entered the small cloak hall with its coat hooks and low shelves for lunch pails. Two swinging doors led into the main classroom with green walls and yellowed white woodwork. Four windows on the

Carney High School, Carney, Okla., was built in 1910. The students pose on the front steps.

north and south walls provided light. I learned later to stay away from those windows, as cold winter breezes found their way through the many cracks and crevices.

In the front of the large room on a raised platform were a teacher's battered desk, a straight chair, a tin book cabinet and several open bookcases. When I searched the cabinet I found a few textbooks and workbooks for my 14 students in grades one, three, four, five and six. We would have to order more supplies, I could see that.

The only items in that schoolroom that worried me were the upright piano and a huge pot-bellied stove. Though I had taken countless piano lessons, I could not play. However, one of the older students could play most songs with one hand and several simple songs using both hands. We "wore those out" as we sang them every day.

The stove proved to be a formidable opponent. I knew nothing about building a fire, keeping it ablaze, or banking it for the night. Dad came to the rescue, though. Either he or Mother drove me to school each morning and picked me up in the late afternoon. He took me on cold mornings, and brought along wood and cobs to build a fire in the stove. We tried to bank the fire overnight but without success.

That stove terrified me time after time. If I was busy and failed to adjust the damper, its belly glowed red with heat. On the other hand, if I forgot to feed the monster, we were all chilled through before I was aware of the problem. On cold mornings the students slid back their rows of desks to surround the old stove. Later, as the heat began to circulate, they moved forward, away from the intense heat.

In the days remaining before the beginning of the school term, I made a daily schedule, reviewed textbooks and designed worksheets. If I wrote with a special purple pencil on white paper, I could duplicate that sheet. I placed the master copy on the sticky gelatin surface in a flat tray, left it to set for a few minutes, and then slowly peeled it away.

After that first sheet, I could make eight or 10 copies by placing clean sheets of paper one by one over the gelatin mixture. If I needed to duplicate a different sheet, I had to wait until the purple writing sank into the gelatin. This proved to be a satisfactory method for making a few copies. One day, however, I left my tray of gelatin in the back window of the car. What a melted mess!

That first morning of school, I arrived early, ready and willing to start my new career. Looking back now, I don't know why I didn't use a truck to transport everything I needed at school. A 5-gallon cream can of water added to my school supplies.

I hauled water to school from our farm because the school's well water had not passed the state health requirements for years. This was not surprising, as the well was located below the outhouses at the bottom of a small hill.

Traipsing up the hill carrying everything was an exercise in physical labor. Soon, however, everything was ready, and parents and children began arriving. I had everything under control until a mother and a small boy wearing glasses arrived. As the mother tried to leave, the boy began screaming hysterically, grabbing his mother's dress and hanging on for dear life.

Being new at the teaching game, I let the mother handle the situation. But when she began to cry, too, I moved forward and tried to reason with the crying, red-faced child as tears streamed down his face and spittle sprayed from his mouth. Finally the mother and child both left, but she assured me that they would return the next day. I was sorry to hear that because the problem was far from being settled.

The next morning, the unhappy scene was repeated. The mother suggested that she attend school with her son, Lloyd. So, during those first weeks of school, I had a visitor whether I wanted one or not. Her presence was unnerving, especially for a young, inexperienced teacher.

Finally, after six weeks, the mother stopped coming to school. I had to lock the school door, however, to keep Lloyd from running home.

Later, in March, the family moved to another school district, but the parents arranged for little Lloyd to ride to school with me. Evidently they didn't want to go through the same harrowing experience with another teacher. Actually, by that time, Lloyd had adjusted fairly well and had become my good friend.

My preparations for becoming a teacher had impressed upon me the importance of supervising and participating in recess activities. I was soon flying across the school yard with my students, daring someone to catch me as we all played dare base.

One day while I was playing second base during a softball game, I caught the ball, then slipped and fell. How embarrassing! Because I was young, I tried to act dignified in all situations. I was even more embarrassed the next day when Rita, the school-board president's daughter, chortled, "Mama said if you had more meat on your bones, you wouldn't fall down!"

One day while we were playing at recess, a car drove up to the school yard and stopped. A well-dressed, middle-aged woman stepped out and walked toward me. I wondered what she wanted. Her first words—directed to me—were "Where is your teacher?"

I drew myself up to my full height, frowned and replied, "I *am* the teacher." She was selling silverware. Needless to say, I didn't buy any.

After school each day I helped children with assignments, cleaned blackboards, dusted and swept the floor. In wet weather I often scrubbed the floor with a rag mop. In cold weather I also carried extra fuel to the schoolhouse. Once I reached home, I had lessons to prepare for the next day and other lessons to correct.

I earned $135 dollars a month but took home $120. I saved most of it, planning to return to college the following year so that I could improve my teaching with more education. My first month's salary, however, went to my parents, who had encouraged and helped me. I appreciated them so much that I used my first earned money to buy each of them something special.

That first school year went by quickly, as I was extremely busy. I had little time to relax, but I enjoyed the children and was delighted when they learned. In that small rural school there was a spirit of caring and love for each other. More than once, one student who had more food than he could eat offered some to several boys who brought plain bread without any sandwich filling. Older students helped younger ones learn math principles and study for spelling tests.

The next year I enrolled in college while my mother took over my job at Center School. As soon as I completed my college degree, I happily returned to teaching. I taught in classrooms for 44 years, always enjoying students and helping them learn. Now, thinking back, I regard teaching as the love of my life. ❖

A Lasting Lesson

By John Oliver

My favorite teacher at Adams Grade School in Seattle was Mrs. Coleman. Tall, with bobbed hair in the fashion of the 1920s, she was serious and strict, but kind, so we gave her respect because we liked her.

Mrs. Coleman taught fourth grade. I remember her mostly from her teaching us the multiplication tables. But what is indelibly carved in my mind—and even more deeply in my heart—is an experience when Mrs. Coleman and I parted company. If I was in the fourth grade, I must have been 10, so the year must have been 1930.

She made me stay after school this particular day for some misbehavior. I had a knack for activity that required disciplinary measures. But this happened to be a very special day. You see, I was also taking piano lessons, and I was scheduled for a lesson that same afternoon.

Now, piano lessons weren't my favorite activity, not by a long shot, but on this day, that lesson loomed as the mandatory requirement in my life. I had to honor it. My character would be ruined if I didn't attend! But there I was, trapped in a second-floor classroom with two or three other kids. What a dilemma! However, Mrs. Coleman herself solved the problem. She left the room. We were alone, unguarded.

By this time I had magnified my piano lesson to crisis proportions. I just *had* to go. So, seconds after she left, I bounded out of my chair and desperately began scouting for escape routes. From the second floor, the ground seemed miles away. No escape there. But then I spotted the drainpipe running from the roof to the ground. Best of all, it was within reach.

Furtively I looked around, fearing that Mrs. Coleman would catch me out of my seat. Fortunately she was still absent. In my panicked state, I don't remember coming to a well-thought-out decision. Let's face it—I simply didn't want to stay cooped up after school, and the piano lesson was my excuse. Now was action time.

I pushed open the window and climbed out. Shinnying down the drainpipe was no problem. In seconds I was on the ground, running pell-mell from the building. In the classroom behind me the other students gasped at my foolhardiness.

In the classroom the other students gasped at my fooshardiness.

The piano lesson turned out to be finger practices or something like that. Dreary.

I really hadn't expected much more; a piano lesson is a piano lesson is a piano lesson.

The next day, Mrs. Coleman didn't speak to me. She didn't call on me for any answers, and she paid no attention to my timid smiles. For all intents and purposes, I had ceased to exist—until the end of the day. Then she took me aside.

I forget all that she said, except for the few words that are still engraved on my psyche, and the calm, firm way she spoke them: "I don't speak to little boys I can't trust."

That was the end of it. No scolding. No lecture. The next day was back to normal. She bore no grudge. I'd been given a reprieve.

As the years rolled on and I graduated from high school and went on to college, I saw Mrs. Coleman from time to time, on the street or in a store. She was always friendly. She was one of those old-time teachers who cherished their students, and never really forgot any of them.

But that confrontation wasn't the end of my escapade. Mrs. Coleman had said her piece, and never required an explanation or apology from me. Yet the experience has never really left me. My conscience continues to do its work. It chastises. I remember the whole episode. I'm 80 now; I was 10 then. That's 70 years of teaching "I don't speak to little boys I can't trust."

I never learned a more lasting lesson. ❖

SCHOOL BUS
JOHN FALTER

School Bells & Buzzers

Chapter Two

Grandma Stamps' home was our getting-on and getting-off point for several school years from the time I was about 10 years old. Times were tough, and Mama had taken a job as a seamstress to augment our family's meager income, so it was only natural that her mother, who lived about a quarter-mile away, would watch us kids before and after school.

Tardiness at the bus stop was not a laughing matter.

And so, every weekday morning found older brother Dennis, little sister Donna and I trekking down to Grandma's to await the arrival of the school bus.

I always envied my schoolmates who lived close enough to walk to and from school. In my adolescent mind, I figured they were able to lollygag a good 30 minutes longer than we country bumpkins could—and those town kids probably didn't have any cows to milk before school either. Yet it seemed that, if there was anyone late to class it was always one of those same town kids.

In all my school years, I was never late for a single bell or buzzer—not that I deserved any credit for that. Early morning chores followed by a hearty breakfast and then a brisk walk to Grandma's bus stop ensured my perfect record.

In warm months, we three played in Grandma's front yard while keeping our eye on the roadway. If we were quiet, we could hear the bus even before it came into view, but we were seldom quiet enough for that. Instead, our first warning was a flash of yellow paint topping the hill above Grandma's just a few hundred yards away. Then it was a mad dash to get to Grandma's mail box, because that was where the bus would stop.

In winter months, it was a bit more complicated. We usually remained inside Grandma's house and watched for the bus through the small window facing south. It was even more difficult to keep our attention focused, yet doubly important to stay vigilant, since we had even farther to go before the bus slowed to a stop.

Tardiness at the bus stop was not a laughing matter. If you weren't waiting to step on when the bus door swung open, there would be no plaintive honking to encourage you to come along. We knew if we were late, we would be left behind. Period. Then you wouldn't be tardy, you would be AWOE—Absent Without Excuse.

If that happened, there would be sure retribution. First it would come from Grandma—who didn't want a bunch of kids to complicate her day—and then from our parents at the end of the day. I never feared schoolmarm or principal the way I did Daddy and his peach limb.

My years on that rural bus route taught me valuable life lessons. I learned about responsibility. I learned about punctuality. And I learned how a good time in the 100-yard dash could keep you out of trouble.

School bells and buzzers—they didn't just let us know when we were tardy. They called us to days filled with the wide-eyed wonderment of learning—days when the schools of our youth taught us so much more than readin', writin' and 'rithmetic.

—Ken Tate

Facing page: *Waiting for the School Bus in Snow* by John Falter © 1947 SEPS: Licensed by Curtis Publishing

First Day of School

By Doris I. Matlock

My first day of school! I was so excited! It was Sept. 4, 1944. My daddy walked with me up to the one-room rock schoolhouse. It was a quarter-mile from my grandpa's big white farmhouse, where we lived. Mama, Daddy, my sister, my three brothers and I all lived on their farm near Tahlequah, Okla.

Mama had made me a new dress for my first day of school. It was cotton material with big flowers in fall colors—brown, yellow and orange—on a green background. I had new shoes, too, and my long hair was all slicked back and braided into pigtails. Daddy took me to school to enroll me because Mama was at home with my baby brother.

I held Daddy's hand tightly as we walked with some other children into the schoolyard. It was all so big and new to me. Our school had been built about 1936 by the Works Progress Administration (WPA), a government program of the Depression era. The building was made of sandstone. The stones had been brought there in horse-drawn wagons by workers from the surrounding hills. It still stands today, sturdy and strong.

I held Daddy's hand tightly as we walked into the schoolyard.

I loved that school. Going through those doors was like entering a magic kingdom. I soaked up knowledge like a big sponge. I developed a love of reading and writing that has helped me through many a tough situation.

Our one teacher kept good order in all eight grades. We younger children were seated in the front of the room so she could help us more. Sometimes she selected some of the older students to help us with reading and arithmetic. We had one teacher for all eight grades until about 1948, when two teachers were hired: one for the first through fourth grades and one for fifth through eighth.

At home we had only a few farm magazines and newspapers to read, so the charts, books and number cards at school fascinated me. I had never had my own books before I started to school. Mama and Granny had helped me with my ABCs before I started school, but no children's books were available. To this day, the smells of chalk, new books and freshly painted classrooms still bring enchanting memories.

School started at 9 a.m. That gave us country kids time to do our farm chores before walking to school. Morning recess was from 10–10:30. Noon hour was from 12–1 p.m. Most of the kids brought sack lunches, which were stored in a closet with shelves and a screen door. What wonderful aromas wafted through the classroom from that home-cooked food!

Some of us who lived close to the school walked—actually ran—home for lunch. Mama usually had a pot of pinto beans and some corn bread for my brothers, sister and me.

We enjoyed our recesses so much because we had to be very quiet and still during study time inside. The younger boys and girls played hopscotch, marbles, Pop Goes the Weasel, Go In and Out the Window, and jump rope, and it was usually the girls who played jacks on the cement steps. The older children played rougher games like Red Rover, Crack the Whip, Flying Dutchmen, softball and Annie-Over.

Afternoon recess was about 2:30–3 p.m. and school was out at 4 p.m. During those hours in class, our heads were down and we were busy reading, writing and doing arithmetic. The hickory stick stood in the corner, within the teacher's reach. We did arithmetic computation with a pencil and paper. We memorized plenty, too—multiplication tables, English, history, etc.

Each class was called up to recite their lessons and/or listen to explanations and illustrations from the teacher. My best teacher was Mr. Dan Herrington, a fine gentleman teacher. He taught grades five through eight. He loved to tell us stories about real events that made our lessons so clear and relevant.

He made our history lessons so alive and interesting, especially the Civil War period. He and his wife, Mary, and daughter, Beth, traveled through the South many summers and visited lots of Civil War battlegrounds and museums. In the fall, he showed us the brochures and other pictures as we studied from our history books.

Daddy was a member of the school board. In my mind, that was as good as being president of the United States. I reminded the other kids quite frequently that my dad was on the board. On one occasion, I told this in a threatening way to some boys who were bothering me. It must have worked, since I don't remember any more problems with them.

Our classrooms and methods of teaching in the 1940s might be considered primitive today, but the patriotism, discipline and community spirit we learned and experienced within those walls can't be beat. ❖

White Oak School, Cherokee county, near Tahlequah, Okla.

My Journey to School

By Danny McGuire
as told to Donna McGuire Tanner

It was 1950 when I started school. My family lived deep in an offshoot of Willis Hollow, W.Va., near Ansted. My mother, Rachel, was nervous about me walking alone to the one-room Adkins School, where Mrs. Thomas taught all eight grades. I'd have to walk several miles over a rough, rutted road.

Soon, however, my parents realized that I would be walking with a group of boys. I remember most of them, especially Gib Wilson and the Willis brothers.

In dry weather, we arrived at our destination all too soon. The trouble began when the rainy season arrived. Then the creek, which had been almost dry, grew into a gushing, raging river. There was no bridge, so cold water soaked our feet and sometimes drenched us nearly to our knees. Just imagine trying to study with wet, bone-chilling clothes clinging to you. Our mothers didn't like it when we came home covered in mud, either.

I can't remember which one of us boys had the brainstorm, but off into the woods we went, to search for poplar trees. They had the strongest wood. We needed small, straight branches that we could encircle with our hands. The branches had to have forks in the right places, too.

We found the proper branches and cut them to size, with the forks positioned at the bottom for our feet. We each had made a set of stilts. We were ready for that creek now!

The real test came the next morning. Once we figured out how to hang our lunches and books on the handles, we were ready. We crossed the creek without even one wet foot—all except one of us.

One of the boys had decided that stilts were not for him. He had gone out and bought a pogo stick. Let me tell you, I have never laughed so hard as when that stick hit a slick rock, and he fell into that chilly water! We had to fish him out before he drowned.

I will never forget the day that my laughter came back to haunt me. Just as I got into the deepest water, my foot branch broke, and down I went. Now *I* was the one to be rescued.

When we reached the schoolhouse, we propped our stilts outside. One day, though, we came out at the end of the day to find that someone had snitched all of our stilts. We never found the prankster, nor the stilts.

I well remember the look on Mom's face when I arrived home that evening in muddy, soaked clothes.

We boys made another trip into the woods and made more stilts. Even after nearly 55 years, I have never forgotten the fun, the laughter and the journey to school. ❖

Facing page: *Back to School* by Robert C. Kauffman © 1937 SEPS: Licensed by Curtis Publishing
Above: 1945 John Hancock Life Insurance Co. ad, House of White Birches nostalgia archives.

The Four-Mile Walk Home

By Helen Oyakawa

When I began first grade in 1938 in Hawaii, my mother, whose education had been cut off after the eighth grade, was determined that all her children would get the most out of school. That meant that neither my brother, a third-grader who was 18 months older, nor I could ever be absent or tardy. When we had sniffles and sneezes, she spread Vicks VapoRub on our chests. Then she tucked an extra handkerchief in my brother's pocket or my denim bag, and she reminded us to cover our mouths so we wouldn't spread germs.

Once I pointed to red spots on my stomach. She frowned at the spots and chewed her lip. She thought it might be chicken pox. Then she felt my forehead and pronounced me nearly normal. She reasoned that because it was a children's disease, my classmates should get it now. She let me wear pants under my dress. She told me to keep my sweater on all day, and added, "Try not to scratch yourself."

Telling us to take care of each other, she waved goodbye and sent us on our way.

She fortified us with hearty breakfasts: oatmeal or corn flakes and slices of papaya flavored with a squeeze of orange or lemon. When avocados were in season in our garden, she mashed its ripe pulp, mixed it with sugar, and slathered it on pieces of bread. We sipped cups of hot chocolate she made with canned Carnation milk. Telling us to take care of each other and listen to the teachers, she waved goodbye and sent us on our way.

School waited four miles to the east. Before the day was over, we covered eight miles—barefooted, like all Kona children. We made that trip each school day from first to sixth grade. In those Good Old Days, traffic in this rural outpost on the Big Island of Hawaii was light. We always traveled with our brothers, sisters, relatives or friends. We spread ourselves to the middle of the two-lane highway, but at the faintest sound or sight of a car, we slid onto the road shoulder.

After just one or two experiences, I learned to avoid the thorns that lay in wait under the most innocent-looking puffs of pink and purple flowers. I also developed a keen eye for other potential tearjerkers: jagged rocks, splintery vines and bits of glass. One day I used my big toe to test an interesting-looking black liquid that bubbled on the edge of the pavement. It taught me thereafter to stay away from the hot, everlasting, sticky tar.

Every two or three weeks my parents gave my brother and me a nickel—sometimes even a dime—to spend after we were through with school. I fingered my coin hour after hour and dreamed of buying the perfect treat. Choosing wasn't easy. Should I take the doughnut doused with sugar? Or should I pick the *anpan,* a Japanese roll without coating but filled with sweetened red beans?

Deciding on an ice-cream cone was no less difficult. Vanilla, strawberry or chocolate? Sometimes I dithered so long that the storekeeper closed the freezer and waited on other customers.

Then there was that tempting Chinese delicacy made from small dried plums. They were seasoned in such a perfect balance that we called them sweet-sour seeds.

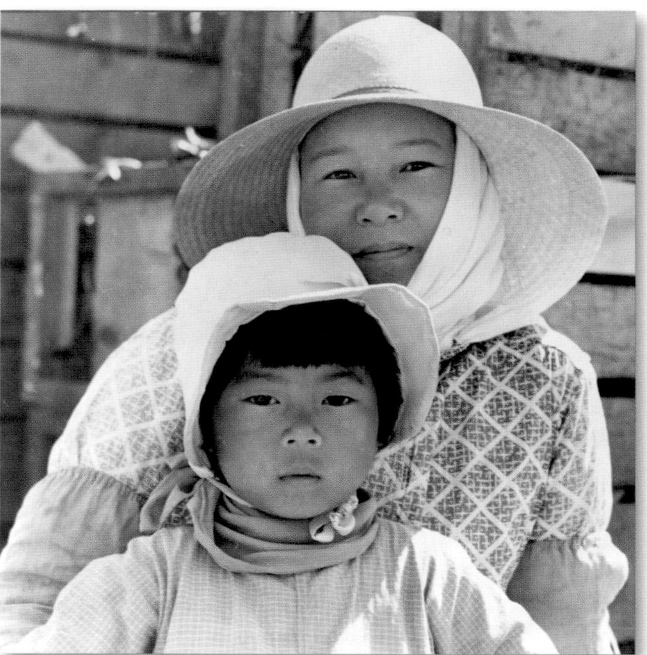

Photograph by Dorothea Lange courtesy the Library of Congress, FSA-OWI Photograph Collection, LC-USF34-016129-C.

Once settling for a pack of spearmint gum, I wondered how they would taste all together. I was disappointed to discover that the flavor of five sticks evaporated just as quickly as that of one lonely piece. Still, I wasn't about to throw away my gum so soon. I stealthily stuck the enormous wad under the table and popped it back in my mouth after supper. I kept chewing it after my mother turned off the kerosene lamp. I hadn't considered that it might fall out, but in the morning, there it was, stuck to my scalp. Unable to pull it out gently, my mother had to resort to cutting it out in patches. That was my worst "bad hair day" ever.

Spending money was not the only way for us to get treats. Two bakeries filled our lungs with the most glorious smells.

We also delighted in the one-room county library. I couldn't believe that I didn't have to pay to look at the books. The white-haired librarian had to assure me more than once that we could borrow as many books as we could carry. These stories, poems and songs enlarged our whole family's life.

The theater—and in particular, *Fantasia,* my first movie—was another source of joy.

My brother and I noted other things on our way to and from school each day. The huge, splendiferous house on the hill was easily three times bigger than the unpainted bungalows on the roadside and behind the acres of coffee trees. We picked up our mail at the post office, said hello to the public health nurse next door, and told each other how much we loved our Christian church built with coral and lava. We shivered at the mysteries of the police station and the pool hall. We wondered what a credit union was—and who used the two banks? We discussed the stores our parents patronized.

I told my brother about a strange lotion that the beauticians used in the beauty shops where our mother and I got our perms. We acknowledged the barbers, the tailor shop, the Buddhist temple, the Kona Electric building, and the markets that sold fish and meats.

By then we were almost home. But first we had to slow down at the pasture to look for ripe thimbleberries, all the time keeping our wary eyes on the cows who lay under the jacaranda or tulip flower trees.

Only then did we begin to run. We were eager to see our mother carrying our baby brother on her back. "Tadaima!" we gleefully shouted. "We're home!" She watched us wipe our tired, dusty feet on a rag outside the door. Then we followed her to the kitchen table where she had placed slices of bread and guava jam and a cup of cocoa.

They were indeed most welcome treats after our long, four-mile walk home. ❖

The Long Road

By V. Frances Hill

In the 1930s, my sister Fern and I attended Clover Hill grade school. Clover Hill was a four-room brick school heated with big coal stoves. The playground, covered with loose dirt, rocks, cinders and ashes from the stoves, must have been the roughest in Rockingham County, Va. Children were always coming to teachers with knees bleeding from a fall. There was also a hollow to the east of the building where grass and straggly saplings tried to grow. But we liked our playground and did not then recognize its deficiencies.

This is a photo of Clover Hill grade school.

We had three routes to the school. Generally we took a shortcut through fields and lanes, a mile or more. The other two ways were called "around the road." There were diversions on the way home. Sometimes we stopped and ate persimmons, or cracked nuts from trees growing in a fencerow. Near an old log dwelling shaded by cedars, we found osage oranges ("hedge apples," we called them) and kicked them partway home. We burst tar bubbles in the paved road.

Other days were more exciting. We crossed a small field on our uncle's farm where three horses galloped wildly, kicking up their heels at us. Once a flock of sheep led by a goat came rushing by, scaring us into finding shelter in our aunt's kitchen. A farmer's bull was sometimes in the road, and we had to hastily climb a fence. And my sister had to hurry past one house because the boys there sang *Sweet Fern* if they spotted her. A ride home was great. When Betty Lee and Alice, our closest neighbors and schoolmates, said their father was coming for us, we stayed around school long after it had closed. A few other children stopped to play ball.

As the evening grew later and colder, a friendly girl put her coat over my shoulders. The janitor, an old man in dark clothes, came to bank the stoves for the night.

Finally the ball game ended and the other children left. We decided to walk toward home around the road so Betty's father could pick us up. Did it enter our minds to walk straight on home? Never! The thought of a ride engrossed us completely.

Along the road we stopped at another log house where Betty had friends. Her father would come for us there, she said. It was dusk when we entered, and the bare hall with a stuffed hawk on a table seemed very lonesome to me. The young woman and her son must have been surprised to see us.

After visiting a little, Betty Lee and Alice started looking out the windows, watching for a car. It was completely dark when they finally saw car lights and announced that their father was coming.

When Fern and I got home, we felt very low. Our usual cheerful homecoming was missing. We were never scolded, however. Our mother and daddy believed it was Betty's fault for leading us on; Betty was older than the rest of us.

Now Fern and I shake our heads when we recall that far-off time and exclaim, "Children! What they can't think of!" ❖

Facing page: 1934 *Farmer's Wife* cover art by Mary Anderson, House of White Birches nostalgia archives

MARY
NDERSON

Nell's Bells

By Dorothy Coleman

Nell stands impatiently waiting for Hanson and me to get settled in the sleigh, stomping her feet from time to time. Every time she paws the ground, the sleigh bells on the harness give off a delightful shudder of sound. Now she shakes her head to show her desire to get moving. This produces another ripple of tinkling bells with a different sound. "Let's go," she seems to say.

The snow swirled down all night. High winds have created drifts in the roads, making it impossible for automobiles to navigate. In 1927, our normal method of transportation to the consolidated high school in the center of the township was by carpool. Not today!

However, we know that Fawn Township High School in southeastern Pennsylvania will be in session no matter what. The principal will be there to open the building, and the 12 students who live in our town will be expected to be there, too.

Good old Nell shakes out bright notes from the bells on the harness.

On snowy days, one of the boys who lives on a farm comes to the rescue by providing a horse-drawn sled that accommodates at least 10 people. We sit on the hay that covers the bottom and cover ourselves with blankets.

The school is only three miles away, but the road is unpaved. Some places have steep banks on both sides with a hollow where the road meanders up the hill. The wind-driven snow has collected here, making it impassable.

On this day, Hanson Street drives up in his one-horse sleigh. Good old Nell, head held high, shakes out bright notes from the bells on the harness. She seems to be in charge. I immediately hop out of the sled and clamber onto the seat before anyone else has a chance. I love riding in a sleigh! It is so much faster and lots more fun. The sound of the bells makes everything sparkle for me.

"Hanson, is it OK if I ride with you?" I ask.

"Sure. We can take the shortcut, going the back way, and be there before anybody else."

"Good!" I settle back with my books and lunch box at my feet and pull the blanket over my lap, ready to go.

I love the sound of the sleigh bells! The bells are part of the harness, and I have the feeling that Nell feels special to be in control of the orchestration of her bells. Right now, as we wait to begin our ride, she seems anxious to get on with the concert.

Finally, Hanson is ready. He picks up the reins, saying, "Come on, Nell, giddy-up." Off we go! Now Nell really has a chance to show off her techniques like a true maestro. As she walks, bobbing her head up and down, she seems to set a marching tempo. She had already shown what she could do as she pawed the ground. Shaking her head gives a ripple that fades quickly.

The sound I like best is when she trots. Then every bell participates, giving constant, loud tinkling—jingle, jangle, jingle, jangle.

We skim over the new-fallen snow at a fast clip, listening to the bells, the wind in our faces. The sleigh's narrow runners seem to whisper and sing along with the tinkling bells. This gray day is now one of exhilaration. Soon we leave our small community behind. The snow is getting deeper, but Nell doesn't seem to mind. She keeps moving at a steady pace, her bells jingling and our spirits soaring.

All goes well until we come to a hill that has steep banks on both sides. Nell moves more slowly now because the snow is getting deeper. The bells quiet to a staccato beat—steady, but not the lively tempo her trotting produces. The wind has driven snow into this pocket between the two banks and filled it. It is beautiful to look at—but impassable.

We see a trackless area that extends from the top of one bank to the top of the bank on the other side of the road. We'll never make it through here. Nell slows to a halt. The bells are silent except for a tiny quaver.

"Hanson, what do we do now? We couldn't even walk in that if we wanted to!"

"Well, I guess we will have to go up the bank and stay in the field until we find a place level enough to get back on the road."

"Can Nell do that?"

"Of course. She is strong, and the sleigh is not heavy. You'll see." Nell obviously puts her mind to the task. She struggles mightily up the embankment, dragging us behind.

Ah, it's steeper than we thought! We almost reach the top and the open field when suddenly, the sleigh lists to one side and tips over. Out into the snowbank we spill—books, lunch boxes and all. Hanson manages to hold onto the reins. It's a good thing he does, because Nell keeps moving along. She clears the top of the embankment and makes it clear that she can keep going, even with the overturned sleigh behind her.

The bells are clanging wildly. Hanson manages to stop her and set the sleigh upright. Then he helps me retrieve the books, lunch boxes and blankets. We shake off as much snow as we can while Nell waits patiently. Still, we look like snowmen as we climb back into the sleigh.

Once again, Nell is in charge of her bells as we regain the snow-covered roadbed. The going is not as easy, but she coaxes sounds from her bells like a true maestro. It is music to my ears!

Hanson still has to unhitch Nell once we reach the stable on the school grounds. He brushes her before he leaves her to come to class. I'm sure he gave her an extra pat.

Sleigh Bells © 2007 by Christine Twomey, used by permission of the artist.

Whenever I hear "Dashing through the snow, in a one-horse open sleigh," it brings back vivid memories of that memorable day in 1927, with Nell and her bells. To this day, the sound of sleigh bells is magical for me. At Christmas, I hang my bells on the front door where they delight me every time one jingles. I often think of Nell, who was able to coax such a medley from her bells. She was a true virtuoso! ❖

MANISCALCO

Papa's Sleigh

By Edna Krause

The best part of winter school days was the three-mile sleigh ride to and from school. Ours wasn't a standard sleigh; it was Papa's special creation. And while Papa was a jack-of-all-trades, a builder he was not. But that didn't matter to my sisters, my little brother, John, and me. We loved the chariot-style box sleigh. But my big brother, Eddie, hated it. In fact, Eddie, the big shot of the Harris High School basketball team, was embarrassed beyond words to ride in it. So while the sleigh kept Papa's young brood warm and happy, he had one highfalutin' senior who was too proud to ride in it.

Only when a storm raged and the north wind piled snow on the roadway did Eddie sit next to Papa on the driver's seat, sharing a black bull hide that they wrapped around their shoulders. We kids huddled under a tarp, well protected by the high boards on three sides of the six-foot-square box sleigh. We sang and laughed as the sleigh's runners hummed over the crisp snow.

Eddie, the big shot of the basketball team was embarrassed to ride in it.

But even on such blustering days, Papa had to stop Prince, the red roan, about an eighth of a mile from school so that Eddie could jump off and walk the rest of the way. Papa waved at Eddie and grinned as though he understood, but we kids said he was nuts to walk when he could ride.

Nonetheless, I was very proud of Eddie, the basketball king, who wore four white stripes on one arm of his maroon school sweater.

I can still see the "H" for "Harris" on his chest. He also wore the latest knee-high leather hightops and dark gray jodhpurs. He bought the clothes with money he earned doing odd jobs.

That January in 1939, when the heavy winter bore down on our farm, Papa threw extra bedding in the chicken coop. While he was at it, he forked a thick layer of hay into the sleigh.

The next morning, we kids yelped with joy when we saw the soft, sweet-smelling hay in the sleigh. We snuggled into its warmth and covered our heads with the tarp, snug as chicks under their mother's wing. I knew that Eddie planned to ride with us when he bellowed, "How am I going to walk into school with straw sticking out of me in every direction like a porcupine?"

Papa said, "This is hay. It won't stick like straw." That seemed to quiet Eddie. He wiggled his feet into the hay and adjusted the bull hide over his knees as he sat with Papa.

We were about halfway to our hilly schoolyard when Papa discovered that there was a problem with the way he had built his sleigh. As Prince cut a sharp corner at a good trot, the sleigh suddenly started to

Facing page: *Dashing Through the Snow,* House of White Birches nostalgia archives

ride on only one runner, throwing hay and all of us to one side. Only Papa's quick thinking saved us from a nasty spill. "Whoa, whoa!" he yelled, pulling the reins. He grabbed Eddie and they slid to the right of the sleigh. "Guess I made the runners too long," Papa confided to Eddie.

From then on, it seemed that Prince saved his swiftest pace for a good, sharp curve. Then he whipped his tail into the air and picked up speed. But Papa always hung on to the reins and slowed him. Eddie still preferred to walk to school whenever winter loosened its icy grip, but how the rest of us enjoyed that sleigh!

The week of the basketball tournament, the mercury dropped below zero and the fierce Upper Michigan wind froze everything in its path. Eddie actually asked Papa to drive him to school to catch the bus for the tournament game.

Because of the deep, drifting snow and the sharp wind, Eddie decided to ride the sleigh farther than usual, until the sleigh was much closer to the hilly schoolyard.

But when he saw the bus off in the distance, waiting in the schoolyard, with people milling around it, he jumped off. Papa continued toward the bus, looking for a place to turn around.

The coach and bus driver came running toward Papa. "Can we use that hay?" called the driver. "We're stuck."

"Go ahead, use it," Papa said.

"Team, come carry some hay!" the coach yelled. "We have a bus to free!" They spread hay around each bus wheel and over icy patches on the slope. Then the driver climbed behind the wheel and shifted into low gear—and, slowly, eased the bus out of its icy prison. A wild cheer rose, and the team crowded around Eddie. His best friend said, "Good thing your dad came along with that sleigh full of hay."

Papa beamed with satisfaction as he watched Eddie and the team get on the bus and leave for the game. Needless to say, never again was the star of Harris High School too haughty to ride in Papa's sleigh. ❖

Winter Sleigh Ride by Walter Emberson Baum © 1937 SEPS: Licencsed by Curtis Publishing

One-Room Days

By Marion Gilmore

In September 1917, my mother, who lived with her family on a 100-acre farm in Dallas County, Iowa, harnessed a pony to a cart and took me, a 5-year-old, a half-mile down a dirt county road to my first day in school. Ours was one of several white clapboard schoolhouses that were built about three miles apart throughout the county on three-acre sections of land. This schoolhouse was built in the shape of a rectangle with large windows on one side and a solid wall on the opposite side to provide for six sections of chalkboard (blackboard).

On one end of this one-room building was a lean-to shed. It held fuel for a coal-burning iron stove that furnished some heat on the very frigid winter days. At the other end, space was partitioned off for a cloakroom and a stand for a water bucket with a dipper. Two outhouses were located at the rear of the schoolhouse yard.

My teacher was a girl who recently had graduated from high school at Minburn, Iowa. She roomed with a family whose children were students at the one-room school. Usually she stayed with the family of the school district's director. Her salary was $70–$80 per month, with room rent at $30 per month.

She walked to school at least two hours early each morning in order to have a blazing fire in the stove before she rang the school bell to begin the day. She also performed some janitorial work—sweeping, arranging the books and papers on the four rows of desks, and washing the chalkboards. The sand table also had to be cleaned and raked. Some years, older students would come early to help sweep the floors.

There were eight grades with 12–15 students in this one-room building. Much of the learning was accomplished with memorization. The first year I learned the letters (alphabet), numbers (addition and subtraction) and colors (primary). Older students read stories to the lower grades, listened to the multiplication tables, and wrote lesson materials on chalkboards.

We enjoyed two 15-minute recesses. The older students played tag as the younger ones ran around the building. Dodge ball was played on the lawn. When the weather was bad, we played checkers, and the older students cranked up the phonograph to listen to favorite music.

My teacher was a girl who recently had graduated from high school.

Our library consisted of two shelves of books along the side wall—*Tom Swift, Rover Boys* and a dictionary.

The teacher planned two programs each year—a Christmas program, and a box social at Easter. All students participated in the Christmas program, presented on the last afternoon before vacation. Parents attended the one-hour program, too.

The box social included everyone, and was held at noon hour on the day before spring vacation. Parents, students and teacher brought decorated boxes to school to sell and then ate together. The teacher's box was specially decorated and brought $2–$4. A hired man from one of the farm families often bought the teacher's box.

The money we raised was used to buy items such as encyclopedias, balls for the playground and library books.

May Hill, the county superintendent at the Adel, Iowa, courthouse, held an eighth-grade examination and spelling contest for all students who had completed eight years in a country school and who wanted to be certified to enter high school.

Today I am 94 years old, and retired after serving as a school principal for 21 years. I graduated from a one-room, eight-year country school with what I needed to live successfully in this very complex and technological world. ❖

April Fool

By Dorothy Stanaitis

As I watch the caravan of buses, SUVs and cars drop children off at our local elementary school, I marvel at how different it all is from the peril-filled trips I made to second grade at James Rhoades School in Philadelphia during the 1940s. Each morning I faced a series of terrifying obstacles, and it took all the courage I could muster to overcome them. Fortified by a goodbye kiss from my mother, I would bravely set off on my block-and-a-half walk to school. I refused to worry her with my problems, so she never knew what I had to endure each day. Still, she would wait on the front porch until I reached the lamppost in the middle of the block where I would turn and wave a final goodbye. Then she would go into our house, and I would face my morning trials.

The first challenge was the neighbor's dog, Brownie. He was tied to their front porch railing each morning, and flew into a frenzy of leaping and barking as I scurried past. I worried that his chain would snap or the porch railing would break, unleashing the menacing, 12-pound ball of fury. My heart pounded as I raced by their house. And I had to do that racing so carefully, jumping and leaping down the sidewalk.

I had just half a block to go to the safety of the school playground.

The neighbors smiled as they watched the little girl they thought was trying some fancy hopping and skipping. They couldn't know that my curious gait was devised to avoid damaged pavement. After all, every second-grader knew that if you stepped on a crack, you'd break your mother's back. And if you stepped on a line, you'd break your father's spine. This hopping, skipping and dodging had to be speedy, too, because every second-grader also knew that if we were late for school, we would be sent to the forbidden corner of the school basement—the janitor's room. There we would be beaten with a cat-o'-nine-tails. We knew this because the sixth-graders had told us so.

When I reached the corner where I had to cross the street, my vigilance increased. We seldom saw traffic go by since most of our neighbors had put their cars away for the duration of World War II. Still, I carefully checked both ways two times before racing madly to the other side of the street.

Then I had just half a block to go to the safety of the school playground, which was surrounded by a six-foot wrought-iron fence. Once inside that fence, the only problem I might have would be my classmates' teasing if I had lost one of the ribbons that tied the ends of my braids, inelegantly called "pigtails" on the playground.

1956 *Wee Wisdom* cover art, courtesy Janice Tate

But one Saturday morning, my mother came into my bedroom and shook me awake, gently but urgently. "Dorothy," she said, "the school called. They're having special classes today."

I looked at the clock, flew out of bed, got ready and dashed out of the house. If I didn't speed to school, I would have to face the janitor's wrath for being late. I never hurried as quickly as I did that day. Leaping and jumping over the sidewalk cracks, I ran past barking Brownie. When I reached the lamppost, I stopped for the usual goodbye wave to my mother.

But instead of waving, my mother was beckoning to me, calling me back to her. What could she want? If I went back, I would surely be late for school. But how could I disobey my mother? I ran back home as quickly and carefully as I could.

Panting and out of breath, I ran up our porch steps. When I reached her, my mother hugged me and laughed. "April Fool!" she said. I stared at her. I couldn't believe my luck. I wouldn't be late for school after all. I wouldn't be sent to the janitor. I was safe at home with my mother.

It was just a joke, an April Fool joke.

Later, I overheard my mother telling her friends about it. She kept saying how glad she was that I hadn't been angry. She said I was a good sport. I was willing to take credit for sportsmanship, but it had really been simple relief that made me laugh so hard at her practical joke on that long-ago April Fool morning. ❖

But more than the teasing, I dreaded the look on my mother's face as she took a few coins from her change purse and sent me once again around the corner to Diamond's Dry Goods to buy a replacement ribbon. Mrs. Diamond knew me by name from my frequent visits.

How I looked forward to Saturdays, when I could take a break from those weekday terrors. Relieved of the fear of crippling my parents by a careless misstep, I helped my mother dust the living room as we listened to one of our favorite radio programs, *Grand Central Station, Crossroads of a Million Private Lives.* In the afternoon, I could go roller-skating with my friends or join the crowd at the Frolic or Belmont movie theater for the matinee. Saturdays were always stress-free and fun.

Writing & the Creek

By Charles C. Walther

The grade school I attended during the 1930s was located in Norwood Park Township, a suburb of Chicago. It was a small school by today's standards; as I recall, enrollment varied from 100–125 students. The school had six rooms, and several teachers taught more than one grade. Thus I was privileged to have the teacher who taught fourth and fifth grades as my mentor for two years.

She was a wonderful teacher who demanded dedication to learning and appropriate behavior at all times. She was very meticulous and seldom overlooked the smallest detail. We loved her even though we sometimes failed to live up to her high standards, academically and behavior-wise.

As fourth-graders in the 1930s, we were introduced to ink and cursive writing. Ballpoint pens had not yet been invented, so we used a nib holder with a changeable nib. It required frequent dipping into an inkwell when we were completing assignments requiring ink.

Most girls screamed whenever an "icky" frog was thrust at them.

Fountain pens had been invented, but our teacher would not allow us to use them. Besides, few students owned one. In the 1930s, a fountain pen was a special gift, reserved for a birthday present or reward for a special accomplishment.

Our teacher made us practice penmanship several times a week. The nib holder with its changeable nib had to be dipped into the inkwell frequently during these exercises. We drew circles, slanting lines and cursive letters on lined paper, over and over. The goal was to achieve writing excellence and qualify for the Palmer penmanship award. Then a certificate was endorsed by Teacher and ceremoniously presented, with all classmates present. Though we spent many hours practicing circles and slanted lines, several members of our class never did earn the certificate.

In the 1930s, our school desks were large and fastened together along the bottom in straight, stable rows with a board on each side. Each desk had a storage area for supplies under its top. The top had a wide pencil groove in the center and a hole in the upper right-hand corner for holding a clear glass inkwell. Our teacher was very conservative. She instructed us to put only enough ink in the inkwell to complete a particular assignment. Otherwise, she insisted that we keep our inkwells clean. We had to wash them out between uses.

Our rural school was surrounded by pastures. Cows often grazed near the school when classes were not in session. During recesses and

lunchtime, we often played in the surrounding fields. A small creek flowed through the field north of the school. Though it was technically off-limits, many students played in it and near it. The inevitable horseplay usually resulted in wet, muddy shoes, stockings or trousers.

Whenever a frog jumped out of the water, several boys would scramble to catch it. Then they would use it to tease some of the fair maidens of our class. Most girls thought frogs were "icky" and screamed whenever one was thrust at them.

In fact, a boy usually teased the girl he was "sweet on."

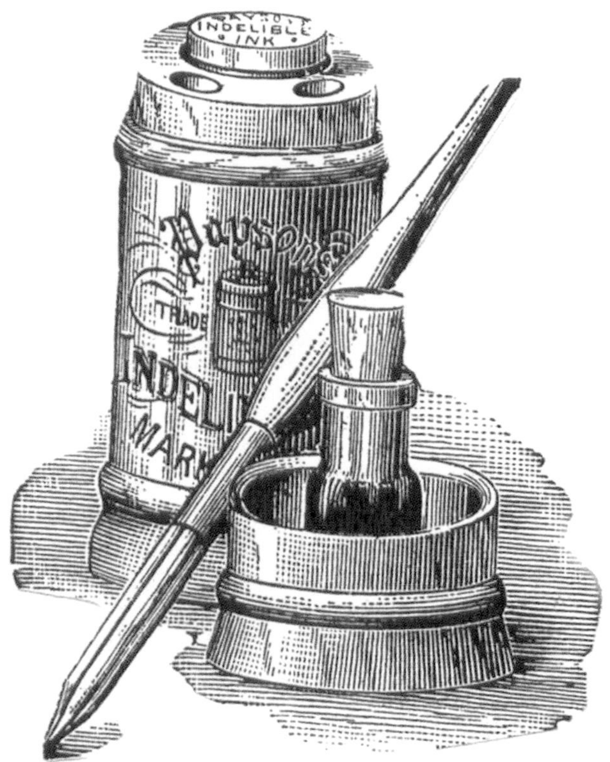

Besides frogs and the occasional turtle, the creek was home to many little crayfish. About a half-inch to an inch long, they paddled about in the water or crawled in the mud on the bottom. Because they were easy to catch, they were also used to tease classmates.

One day, Alex suggested that after scrubbing our inkwells, we should fill them with water and put one of the small crustaceans in them. "We can have our own aquarium and special entertainment," he emphasized. Several of us enthusiastically endorsed his plan.

In anticipation, we diligently cleaned our inkwells after the last writing exercise. We were excited; soon we would have our own aquariums complete with star performers.

On the day of the big event, Teacher must have thought her mischievous charges had finally reformed and recognized the wisdom of her many lectures concerning behavior and spotless inkwells. Our behavior was exemplary.

Time dragged as we anticipated the coming event. Activities were confined to studies, with only an occasional snicker, smile or smirk. Notes were seldom passed, and few paper wads zipped across the room. There was little laughter and few guffaws if a classmate goofed.

When recess finally came, we went directly to the creek. All the boys involved in the escapade captured one of the little critters. Though they struggled to escape, we held them gently in the palms of our hands as we returned to class.

During the melee as we returned to the classroom and took our seats, we introduced our captives to their new homes in our water-filled inkwells. They floated, swam or languished on the bottom. If they had feelings, they were probably devastated because they no longer were free to swim about or burrow into the mud. But we enjoyed our new seatmates.

All of the culprits who had kidnapped one of the creatures demonstrated extra diligence and dedication to learning—for a time. We busied ourselves with lessons and hid behind our books to observe our little charges' antics. Teacher probably thought she was dreaming that afternoon. Her little pranksters conducted themselves as model students. Perhaps—at last!—her many lectures concerning proper behavior and dedication to learning had finally worked their influence on us.

All went well until one aquarium manager decided to place his little "seatmate" on his desktop and watch it crawl when he prodded it with a pencil. Then one of our more squeamish classmates noticed and loudly proclaimed, "Teacher, some of the boys have icky crabs on their desks!"

Teacher stopped grading papers and stood up. When she observed what was happening, she shouted, "What have you done? What are you doing? Who told you that you could bring crabs into the classroom and put them in your inkwells and on your desks?"

Some of the more timid classmates cowered in disbelief; they had never heard Teacher shout or seen her so angry before. Of course, most of us had experienced her wrath previously, when being chastised in the hall or while being escorted to the principal's office.

As soon as Teacher identified the participants in the crab escapade, she marched us outside to the creek. She stood by and watched as we reluctantly returned our visitors to their natural habitat. Returning to our classroom, she made us stand in front of the blackboard, facing our classmates.

Standing off to the side, she lectured and chastised us again. She emphasized that we had frightened Rosette, Geraldine, Ingrid, Mildred and other members of our class. When one of the culprits snickered, she let loose a second, more forceful lecture. Finally she made us promise that we would never again bring crabs, frogs or snakes into class. Our classmates watched as we promised to obey the rules and meekly returned to our seats.

After school, we all met and confided that we had had our fingers crossed when we made that promise to Teacher. Back in the 1930s, children agreed that when you crossed your fingers when you made a promise, you were not obligated to keep it. It was our way of beating the system. ❖

Down Memory Lane

By Tena Bartels

Will you take a walk with me,
And go down memory lane?
Pretend that you're a child again—
You have so much to gain.
Let's take the path along the way
That leads to home sweet home—
The place we lived when very young
With memories alone!

Let's walk that lane to school again
When everyone was glad;
With a lunch bucket in my hand
And running hoops ahead.
We had such fun along the way,
It didn't seem long at all,
Although we walked a mile or two
When starting school in fall.

We sat on wooden benches
Around an old coal stove;
Although our feet were very warm
We almost froze our nose!
The teacher spoke in quietness;
We could hear the old clock tick;
No one ever talked out loud
Or we would think them sick.

We studied hard and really learned
About the Golden Rule.
We listened to each other speak;
Those were great days at school!
What a pleasant sight it was
To watch each class recite;
Each tried to beat the other
And prayed that all was right.

In memory I can recall
Those happy days of old
When everyone was anxious
To praise instead of scold.
They are precious memories
That years cannot erase;
We love to once again recall
That special, hallowed place.

Isn't it just wonderful,
That God gave us a mind
To store away these memories
So later we can find …
Many happy thoughts again
To reminisce awhile
And think of those days gone by
When we were but a child?

GEOGRAPHY

Tom's School

By Paul Huling

I'll never know if it was Tom's mother or my mother who conceived the idea that when the public schools in LaSalle, Ill., had days off, that would be a good time for me to visit the Robinson farm north of town. Tom was—and still is—my good friend. If I visited him on a day that he had school, Tom went off to school with me in tow.

At first I thought that was going to be the pits, visiting a one-room country school where one teacher taught all grades. I'll spend the whole day with nothing to do but wait, I thought.

How wrong I was! After the first time or two at Tom's school, I actually looked forward to going!

I liked to go because I learned so much. The upper-grade students were not condescending; on the contrary, they were helpful to the lower grades, and the little kids looked up to them with great admiration.

All eight grades helped each other. The school was a unit where each student cared for the others. I had never been in a school like that.

Nellis School, District 176, north of LaSalle, Ill., and south of Bauers. Front row (left to right): Thomas Robinson—my friend Tom, Doris Crane, Don Freebairn, Anna Jean Freebairn, Lorraine Johnson, Roth Hill, Richard Dudek, Eugene Dugosh. Back row (left to right): Wayne Black, Wesley Freebairn, Tom Freebairn, Lorraine Crane, teacher Martha Rogowski, Lorretta Crane, Lucille Hill, Wes Black, Leo Dugosh.

Getting to school was another experience. Instead of walking brick sidewalks as I did in town, Tom and I walked through the woods and fields along the creek. Some days, when the creek was too swift to cross, we walked the gravel road for about a mile.

One time, on our walk through the woods, we came upon an opossum that was "playing 'possum." When we described it to Tom's father, he told us what it was. We returned to the spot where we had seen it, and sure enough, it was gone.

In winter, we would arrive at the school to find that the teacher had already fired up the wood-burning stove to warm the room.

No wonder Tom's so smart, *I thought.* He'll hear this lesson eight times over! ***And I only got to hear the lesson once; was that fair?***

Tom's teacher never minded my visits. I wished she had been my teacher a time or two.

All students stood facing the flag for the Pledge of Allegiance. Then each class would take its turn to go to the front of the room where the students sat on the bench for their lessons. Everyone in the room could hear—and learn.

No wonder Tom's so smart, I thought. *He'll hear this lesson eight times over before he graduates.* And I only got to hear the lesson once; was that fair?

One day, lo and behold, the whole school had a geography lesson at once. First-graders at Tom's school could find Cuba on a world map. Eighth-graders could find cities like Belem (in northern Brazil). No wonder Tom had fun with me, talking geography. I was a dummy compared to kids at his school.

All in all, I'd say Tom received the superior education when we were growing up. It wasn't that I attended an inferior school; it was just that I was a boy who would have done better at his school than I did at mine. ❖

Some Wishes Do Come True

By Nettie Gornick

In the mid-1930s when I was 10 or 11 years old, I attended an elementary school in Springdale, Pa. When I walked to school, I took a shortcut across the railroad tracks. The train had stopped running there many years ago.

When I entered the classroom, I noticed activity around the teacher's desk. As I moved closer, I saw a box full of Red Cross buttons on her desk.

Some of the children were giving the teacher their pennies and pinning the buttons onto their shirts and dresses. I knew I had to have one of those buttons so I could help the Red Cross in my own little way.

When I ran home for lunch that afternoon, I told Mama about the Red Cross buttons and asked if she could please give me a penny to buy one. Mama said she was sorry, but she didn't have a penny to give me. I was crushed. Tears welled up in my eyes.

As I trudged back to school across the railroad tracks, I felt sad because I could not help the Red Cross. I closed my eyes tightly for a second and wished hard that I had a penny—just one penny.

Suddenly, as if prodded, I looked down on the ground. To my great surprise, there was a penny! I could not believe my eyes!

I picked it up and clutched it in my hand. Putting my hand into my jacket pocket, I held on to it tightly so it wouldn't get lost.

Happily, I ran the rest of the way to school. As I entered the classroom, I hurried to the teacher's desk, smiling broadly, and gave the teacher my penny. She handed me a Red Cross button and I proudly pinned it onto my jacket.

Smiling all the way home, I knew in my heart who had put that penny there so a little girl would be happy.

Thank you, Father. ❖

A Dillar, A Dollar, A 9:05 Scholar

By Betty Artlip Lawson

When my high-school career began in 1944, it seemed the entire world was weary. Even the children were worn out from the years of worry regarding the welfare of loved ones in the service of our country. The textbooks on which we paid rental charges that year were worn out and most were out of date as well. Many of our teachers had given up retirement in order to return to a career they had thought finished. They deserved a rest, but most felt their duty lay with the children and their need to be educated, so we began high school with both books and many of our teachers worn out from much prior service.

The only event which made starting high school exciting for me was the chance to meet new classmates. The one-room country school students would have to come to town for their high-school education, and we would have the chance to make new friends. I think there were four in this category in my freshman year—three girls and a boy. One of the girls did become a special friend of mine and remained so for years.

The solemn atmosphere washed away all of my self-assurance.

Nevertheless, my freshman year was frustrating and full of depression. If I seldom missed the honor roll, it was more because there was little of interest in my life to keep me from my books.

The following September was so different. The war was over. We continued to have worn-out books and weary instructors, who surely wished with all their hearts only to get away from these tiresome, active and noisy students, but we knew better times were definitely on the way.

A promise of finer things to come, our own good spirits, and the sight of discharged young men appearing, one or two at a time, in our small town helped us through our sophomore year. I was on the honor roll a bit less that year. There were so many exciting things happening during this year which claimed more of my attention.

September 1946 found me a high-school junior with new books, new, young teachers, and lots of new apparel, the latter finally flooding the market now that the yardage was not all used for the military. The clothing and yardage factories at long last had a sufficient labor force, and new clothing was becoming commonplace. (Also, everyone seemed to have more money to buy such things.)

Our new principal was a recently discharged military man and only 12 years or so older than the senior students. He commanded respect, but we soon learned we could get away with quite a lot if we didn't flaunt our indiscretions. If it were possible for him to ignore our imprudence with no loss of dignity, he would do so. He must have been weary of military discipline and so decided to let us have a certain amount of liberty.

Mostly though, we girls were thrilled with the wavy-haired, blond giant who came to our small high school as coach and history instructor. He was known as "Doc" in the gymnasium and "Mr. S." in the classroom. The "Doc" was because he was merely making a temporary stop with us in order to make the money he needed to complete his education and become a veterinarian.

Doc was probably no more than eight years older than most of us. We soon found out we could get away with a good deal of impertinence while he was in charge of the assembly. ("Assembly" is what we called the room the students of today refer to as study hall or home room.)

I lived only one short block from school; leaving by the rear door, it was closer to three-quarters of a block. I was a member of the first-string basketball team. Because of this, and because some of the returned military men had shown definite interest in the amount of growing up I had done during their absence, I was rather in the way of becoming a show-off.

Along about December of my third year of high school, I was rapidly becoming far too impressed with myself. My mother had a great amount of difficulty in getting me out of bed almost every morning. When this was finally accomplished, I would dawdle until the last possible moment before getting ready for school. I would shoot out of the back door only after hearing the last bell. Consequently, I always slipped into the morning assembly while the student body was in the midst of the flag salute. This was one of the mischievous acts our young principal chose to ignore. He stubbornly refused to see me slipping in late each morning. On the other hand, Mr. S. could hardly pretend he didn't see me, as I had to walk right by him every morning to reach my desk. But I reasoned that if I simply walked by him with a swish of my skirt and head held high, he would not have the heart to make an issue of my impudent behavior.

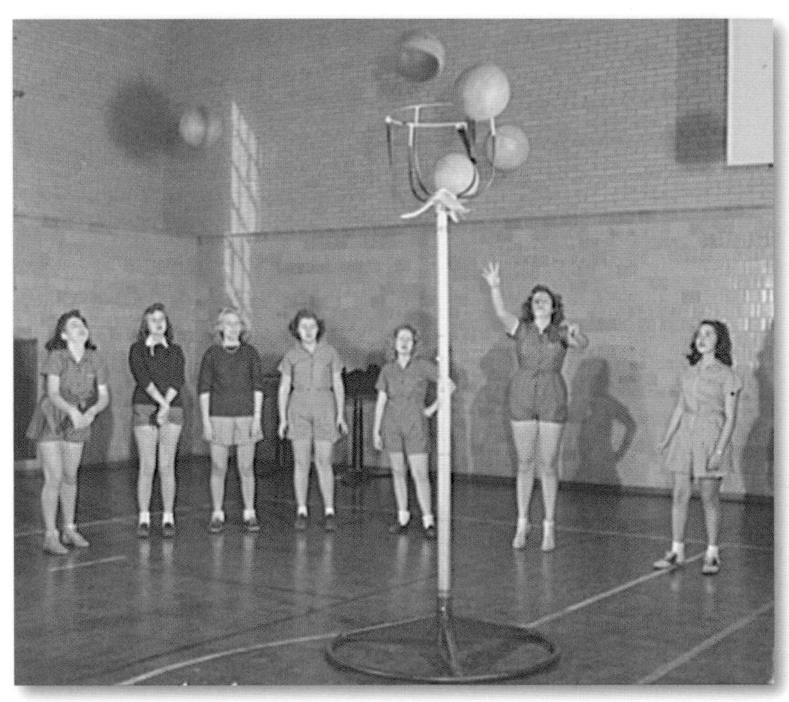

A group of girls practice basketball in a high school physical education class in October 1943. Photograph by Esther Bubley courtesy the Library of Congress, FSA-OWI Photograph Collection, LC-USW3- 039798-D.

I was correct up to a point. At first, only a few of my particular friends would snicker and giggle at my disrespectful behavior. But as my late arrivals continued—and as I continued to swish by Mr. S.—it was forcibly brought to the attention of the entire student body. Later still, it became almost a game to everyone from the janitor and the smallest first-grader on the floor below us to the principal, who was still determined not to see it.

As kids are all too apt to do, I pushed my luck too far in February. Being a bit later than usual and finding the assembly had finished the salute, I sensed at once that my behavior was not to be ignored one day longer. The guffaw my later-than-usual arrival drew from the students was a bit too much even for Doc.

Having been pushed into a showdown, like it or not, Mr. S. was now forced to take action. He said, "Betty, would you come up to my desk, please?"

I had my back to him by this time and was on my way toward my desk. I made an "Uh-oh!" face that our instructor could not see, but the class guffawed in response. It was then that I decided to keep score to make the confrontation more fun. One for me for drawing the laugh—and one more for the facial expression that had entertained my classmates. Doc–0; me–2.

I flipped around in my short, pleated skirt, and without the shadow of a smile, I walked to the instructor's desk. "Did you want me, Sir?"

Mr. S. sighed. "Not really." This made the score Doc–1, me–2.

I stood just behind his desk chair where he could not see what I was up to. I stuck a minute bit of my tongue out and opened my eyes wide, bringing about another lapse of control from the class. Score: Doc–1; me–3.

Doc said, "Betty, will you tell the assembly how far you live from school?"

"Why?" I replied. "They all know me and know where I live." Doc–1; me–4.

Allowing that to go by, he said, "Will you tell the students how many days this week you have been tardy?"

I had a ready answer. "That depends what day of the week this is."

He countered by addressing the company at large: "All together, now, students: What day is this?"

A loud chorus of "Thursday!" and a laugh came back to him, and I mentally noted the tally: Doc–2; me–4.

I defended immediately with, "Monday is one, Tuesday is two, Wednesday is three, so that makes today is four times this week I've been tardy."

Needless to say, my impertinence was duly appreciated. Doc–2; me–5.

At this point, Doc had the great good sense to dismiss me with the promise we would finish our verbal battle later and in private. The students were dismissed to go to their classes. The school day began a bit late, but everyone was in jolly good humor, thanks to the repartee between Doc and me.

I went off to my first class as saucy as ever. I felt confident of my ability to best anyone in a battle of wits. The promise of a later confrontation worried me not at all. It was, in fact, an exciting prospect, as my adversary was a quick wit and a fine competitor.

I didn't know it then, but our meeting was to take place during the last period of the school day. When the assembly attendant told me I was wanted in the principal's office, I merely sharpened my wits, made another of my patented "Uh-oh!" faces at my cohorts, and flippantly exited the assembly.

Expecting to find Doc alone in the office, I was rather perplexed to find our principal there, also. It was apparent that he intended to participate in this interview. The solemn atmosphere washed away all of my self-assurance. The score was suddenly a tie—and Doc was about to score the winning points.

There were quite a lot of words spoken during that horrid interview. It all came down to the question of whether I wished to continue on the basketball team. My answer, of course, was that I wished to do just that. Doc and the principal assured me that if I were to receive a failing mark in citizenship, the team would have to struggle along without me. And, they continued, a failing mark was more than just a possibility, should my tardiness not end immediately.

Need I tell you? The morning following this one-sided interview, I was in the assembly and seated at my desk by 8:45 a.m. For a change of pace, I helped salute Old Glory that morning. As a matter of fact, I was present to participate in the daily salute each morning for the remainder of that year and the whole of the next.

I am ashamed to say that my name was never to appear on the honor roll again. Life was far too exciting. Diversified interests found me unwilling to spend the necessary time on such unimportant things as books. I have regretted this many times over in later years. Oh, my! What fools many teenagers be. ❖

R.B.
CHARLES BERGER

Ditching School

By Bonnie Blunk

When I was a high-school freshman in 1939, I was in childish awe of my brother, Martin, two years older than I, for fearlessly ditching school on a regular basis without getting caught. He had mastered the art of copying Daddy's handwriting so well that even the feared "Pop" Snider, superintendent of Delta High School, could not detect the difference when, after a day of climbing trees and wrestling in the city park with his fellow vagabonds, Martin glibly wrote his own excuses.

Martin did not fear Pop, even though rumor implied that if Pop caught you ditching, he would stand you in a corner facing your class the livelong day without food, make you sweep his office floor with a toothbrush, and much worse. No one seemed to know what "much worse" was, but it was out there, and it was not taken lightly.

Neither did Martin fear Daddy, who, when we were in grade school, had let our teachers know that if we got a spanking at school, he'd give us another when we got home.

"After you graduate, you'll wish you'd had some fun, and it'll be too late."

Martin said it was because I was a girl that I was afraid of everything, and he constantly dared me to ditch. "After you graduate, you'll look back on your dull days in school, wish you'd had some fun, and it'll be too late," he said. "Come on, I'll write your excuse and you won't be caught."

I admitted my fears, but even worse were the waves of shame I felt at the mere thought of getting caught. My best girlfriend, Juanita, didn't help. She occasionally ditched and got away with it, and she was after me to go with her.

She had it all planned. Once off the school bus, we'd sneak off to her sister Esther's house six blocks away, where we would eat breakfast with her family and play with her twin boys.

The afternoon would find us in Holland's women's store, trying on hats—our favorite pastime when we went to town together on Saturdays. Holland's boasted beautiful women's hats—all colors, bedecked with feathers, ribbons and jewels. We had as much use for a fancy hat as a chicken does for a toothbrush, but we did it anyway.

After trying on hats, we would get back to the school bus in time to board and go home without a hitch.

Her plan sounded solid, so I asked Martin to write me an excuse. "I'm proud of you," he said, whipping out his pencil.

I was choking on butterflies when we got off the bus that morning and stealthily made our way to Esther's. But as we ran to catch the

Facing page: *Gone Fishin'* by Charles Berger, House of White Birches nostalgia archives

bus late that afternoon, I hated myself, Martin and Juanita.

It had been a horrible day; nothing had gone as planned. Breakfast was over by the time we arrived at Esther's. She put us to washing dishes while she bathed the twin boys. She let Juanita know that she did not approve of what we were doing, and this made me feel unwelcome.

There was no trying on hats, either; we had to watch the babies sleep while Esther shopped for groceries. And she didn't live six blocks from school; it was 12. The next morning, I had no sooner left my forged excuse at Pop's office and seated myself in my first class than an office clerk appeared at the classroom door. "Bonnie Hubbs is wanted at the office," she called out.

I am 76 years old now and have encountered many a trial in my life, but I do believe that that short walk to Pop's office was the longest I have ever taken. I was dead. I knew I would not get out of his office alive.

To begin with, Pop was a formidable figure. He wore his hair in a crew cut. He was tall, and he had a huge stomach. But the scariest part of him was the stern look that never left his face.

He was seated behind his desk when I timidly entered the room. He motioned for me to sit. The longer he stared, the more frightened I became. My face was burning up; I could feel it turning all shades of red. The only sound in the room was my heart thumping. His fingers began tapping a piece of paper on his desk. As he slowly moved the paper toward me, I knew it was my ill-gotten excuse. But when he spoke, I was bewildered by the softness of his voice.

"Now, Bonnie," he said, "your father did not write this excuse, did he?"

I barely had the strength to shake my head.

"All right," Pop murmured. "You go on back to your class now." And that was the sum of it.

I learned several things that day. The other things the kids said about Pop might or might not have been true, but he was also kind, and a good judge of people. I'm convinced he knew that the shame I was feeling at that moment was all the punishment I needed to keep me from ditching school again. His unexpected leniency made me even more ashamed of myself than I already was when I first entered his office.

I also learned to follow my own instincts and not someone else's, to have the courage to follow my own convictions, and to take responsibility for my own actions. After all, that someone you allow to help you get into trouble is not always going to be around when the consequences are handed out. ❖

Country Schoolhouse

By Delphia Frazier Smith

Have you stopped to listen
To a ringing bell
At the country schoolhouse
That we loved so well?

Children with their lunches,
Hurrying on the way,
Shouts and happy laughter,
On this special day.

The first day of school …
The start of a new year …
Kids with books and paper …
For younger ones, a tear.

Summer days have ended;
It's time to start once more
To the little schoolhouse
With its inviting door.

Faces bright and smiling,
Benches on which to learn;
And a nervous giggle
When it was your turn.

Many years have vanished,
Yet those days I recall,
The cherished days we spent
At the schoolhouse in the fall.

Playing Hooky

By Mary Fulcher

As I stroll down memory lane, one incident in my childhood stands out above all others. My cousin and I had been anxiously looking forward to our first day of primary school.

That beautiful day finally arrived, and we were two very happy little girls. There were lots of children, and I can still smell that old chalk and board, and the sawdust.

The first and second days were just fine, but then boredom set in. My cousin was the first to decide she was ill.

The teacher let her go home, but we lived a mile and a half from school, so a high-school pupil was sent to walk home with my cousin—I suppose to be sure nothing happened to her.

The next day, after getting to spend an afternoon at home with her mom, my cousin was back in school. I thought that if it had worked so well for her, why not give it a try?

And that's what I did the next day. I actually made myself believe my tummy was hurting; maybe if the teacher would let me go home, Mom would give me something to make me feel better.

I will never forget that hot day. After I told the teacher I didn't feel well, she picked a grown girl to walk home with me. But I think the girl doubted me a little from the glances she cast my way. Maybe she thought the heat would get me.

Anyway, we arrived home, and Mom didn't seem too surprised to see me. She thanked the girl for bringing me home.

Then Mom made me lie down on the bed and pulled my shoes off. She got the thermometer, but I had no fever. She said she knew what would help me. She gave me a big spoonful of castor oil, and believe me, if I hadn't been sick before, I was then. That was terrible!

But it really did the trick. I never played hooky again. ❖

School Days

Author Unknown

Nothing to do, Nellie darling?
Nothing to do, you say?
Let's take a trip on memory ship,
Back to the bygone days.
Sail to the old village schoolhouse,
Anchor outside the school door,
Look in and see—
There's you and there's me,
A couple of kids once more.

Chorus:
School days, school days,
Dear old golden rule days,
Reading and writing and 'rithmetic,
Taught to the tune of a hickory stick!
You were my queen in calico,
I was your bashful, barefoot beau.
You wrote on my slate, "I love you, Joe,"
When we were a couple of kids.

'Member the hill, Nellie darling?
And the oak tree that grows on its brow?
They've built forty stories upon that old hill,
And the oak tree's an old chestnut now—
'Member the meadow so green, dear?
So fragrant with clover and maize?
Into new city lots
And preferred business plots,
They're cutting up since those days.

Homeroom Holidays

Chapter Three

Museums were something my class never got to visit when I was a young sprout back in the Good Old Days. Our school was too small and our town too remote to take "field trips" the way the city schools did.

Heck, the only field trips we got to take were to the fields that were producing some kind of food.

I longed to visit New York City and see the great paintings like "Washington Crossing the Delaware" at the Metropolitan Museum of Art. I would have given just about anything to visit the Smithsonian or the Library of Congress.

But those institutions were well over a thousand miles away, and I could count on one hand the number of times we had visited Springfield, Mo.—just 40 miles away—all the years of my childhood.

In fact, after counting those times on one hand, I would still have two fingers left over.

Then along came sixth grade and Mrs. Adams. She was tough, and she was mean, but she had a vigorous exciting way of teaching that built an educational fire under me. Her forte, as far as I was concerned, was history; no other teacher I had could make that subject come to life the way Mrs. Adams could.

We didn't have to see "Washington Crossing the Delaware" at the Met. Mrs. Adams had us building paper boats and coloring colonial flags. We spent a cold, snowy February 21 learning about our first president (Washington's birthday, not "Presidents' Day," was the next day). She even went with us outside at recess, asking us to imagine what it might have been like at Valley Forge.

The only field trips we took were to the fields that were producing food.

Mrs. Adams tied every one of our homeroom holidays to some lesson from history, science or some other subject. Around Armistice Day we learned about "the war to end all wars." Thanksgiving was a time to learn about Plymouth Rock, the voyage of the *Mayflower* and the first feast celebrated between the Pilgrims and their native American benefactors. At Christmas we learned at school, as well as at church, about the birth of the Messiah.

Oh, yes, Mrs. Adams was a historian *and* a religious woman.

So it was that through the hours and days and weeks and months of that 11th year of my life, Mrs. Adams' tutelage taught me one of the most important life lessons of all: If you can read, if you can imagine, if you can dream—you can go anywhere your mind can take you.

I quit wishing I could visit some of those big museums in some of those big cities. Better than a field trip to Springfield, Kansas City or Washington, D.C., that tough and mean country schoolmarm taught me to ride books past all of those intermediate destinations on my way to the world.

These stories of Homeroom Holidays will warm your heart as you go back to those school days of yesteryear.

—Ken Tate

Facing page: *Washington Crossing the Delaware* by Stevan Dohanos © 1951 SEPS: Licensed by Curtis Publishing

xxxx
Be
mine
Anne
Jeff
John
Slobodnik

The Valentine Box

By Dorothy Stanaitis

Shirley Singer's mother made our box. Cardboard was hard to come by during the years of World War II, but the Singers owned a grocery store and had access to all sorts of scarce treasures. The box was large, square and covered with ruffled pink crepe paper and paper lace doilies. Stickers of red hearts, pink roses and lavender lilacs were scattered all over it except where the wide slit had been cut to receive our valentines.

It was the most beautiful box on the second floor of the James Rhoades School, and our class was very proud of it.

The children in 4-B had a valentine box done up like a regular U.S. mailbox, which was clever, but it did not compare to our colorful flight of fancy. 5-A and 5-B had red boxes with lots of white ruffles, but they seemed a little brash compared to our pretty pink confection.

We were sure of it: Our class had the very best box on the second floor of the school.

All week the children had been bringing in penny valentines, which they secretly pushed through the box's slot. No one ever signed those cards, except with a variation of "?" or the cryptic words "A Good Friend." The whole operation had an air of mystery and secrecy, which only added to the suspense and excitement we all felt.

The box was large, square and covered with pink crepe paper.

There were no PTA room mothers planning parties with cupcakes and punch that year. Most hoarded what little sugar and butter they could get for their own family celebrations. So our classroom fete would consist of making valentines to take home to our mothers, singing the three Valentine's Day songs we had practiced, and then the grand opening of the beautiful box and the distribution of its contents.

I had contributed four cards to the box. My mother had given me a nickel to get five penny valentines, but I couldn't resist buying myself a piece of rock-hard fudge for one penny. The harder the fudge the better, we fourth-graders said. The fudge lasted longer that way.

The valentines I did buy were for my two best girlfriends, Doris Hinkle and Shirley Singer, and one for our teacher, Mrs. Morrow. The fourth card was for a boy.

William Stiles would have no idea who "A Good Friend" was, since we had never exchanged a friendly word—or *any* words, for that matter. But I hoped St. Valentine would work his magic, and somehow make William notice the girl who secretly admired him. I even went so far in my imaginings as to picture a large, lacy, 5-cent valentine sent to me by William.

Facing page: *Be Mine Sweet Valentine* by John Slobodnik, House of White Birches nostalgia archives

At last the big day arrived. On Feb. 14, I wore red ribbons tied into bows on the ends of my braids, or "pigtails" as they were called on the playground. Our class was wild with excitement and raced around the playground until the bell rang ending recess and signaling the start of our Valentine's Day celebration.

To tell you I love you
I've often times tried,
But I'm awful bashful
When I'm by your side.

After the laboriously crayoned cards to our mothers were tucked away in our desks and the three holiday songs were sung with great feeling, the teacher chose a small, quiet boy, John Morrow, to be the valentine mailman. John was no relation to Mrs. Morrow, but we all felt that he was her favorite because they shared the same last name.

John pulled the valentines from the box one by one. He haltingly read the names on the envelopes out loud, then took the card to the eager recipient's desk. The suspense was almost unbearable. I watched John deliver the card I sent to Shirley Singer, who let it sit on her desk without opening it. She intended to open all of her cards at once. I hadn't received any cards yet, but I decided to save them all to open at once, too.

John was slow in delivering the cards, and had trouble deciphering the names on the envelopes. He even gave Robert M's card to Robert J. Finally, Mrs. Morrow got up from her desk to help him. She took a handful of cards and began passing them out without reading the names aloud. I saw her deliver two to William Stiles. I wondered if one of them was mine.

Finally, John Morrow came to my desk with an envelope. I recognized the handwriting at once. I knew it was from Doris Hinkle without even opening it.

Mrs. Morrow finished distributing her cards, and John had just four more to deliver. I had received only three so far.

At least one of the cards John was holding must be for me. My heart was pounding. I felt my eyes start to sting with held-back tears. But I didn't get any more cards.

Shirley Singer got six, and Doris Hinkle had five. William Stiles received 10. Mrs. Morrow had 22, but there were 25 children in the class. I wondered who had ignored the teacher. I knew one was Robert J., who had bragged all week that he was too old for babyish valentines and wasn't sending any. None of us figured out that he had no spare pennies to buy cards.

I felt miserable. I couldn't believe I was so unpopular. I thought that more people liked me, but it seemed that they liked rock-hard fudge better. In my disappointment, I never thought about the fact that I had sent only four valentines myself.

But I bounced back from that disappointment quickly and began damage control. I spread my three cards and three envelopes all over my desk to make it look as if I had received more cards than I did. Then I took my No. 2 lead pencil and roughly erased the "?" on the card that I knew must have come from Shirley Singer. Over the smudged erasure, I carefully printed the message, "Love from William Stiles." ❖

Cupid Finally Delivered

By Marianne Bayless

The influence of Jack Frost was still evident as February ushered in the anticipated Valentine's Day. This was a big event for students at the Margaret Park Grade School on Manchester Road in Akron, Ohio.

When I was in third grade, my parents decided I should have store-bought valentines. The big five-and-dime was the place to shop. The teacher said we should give everyone in our class a valentine. My punch-out book had just enough. In curvy letters I wrote my name on the back of each one. At the ripe old age of 8, I thought boys were icky; therefore I did not give much thought as to who got what valentine. But that was soon to change!

By seventh grade, boys were no longer icky and Valentine's Day took on a whole new meaning. This was also the year I graduated from punch-out valentines to the more interesting ones that came in fancy boxes.

My mother still thought I should give everyone in my class a valentine, but I protested. There were some boys in my class to whom I did *not* want to give a valentine; I didn't want them to think I considered them a valentine interest. On the other hand, my best friend and I giggled at the prospect of receiving valentines from those very same boys.

Finally it was time for the party in Miss Mitchell's seventh-grade class. As was traditional, each of us had decorated a shoebox, marked it with our name, and cut a large slit in the top. At the teacher's signal, everyone walked around, checking out the names on the boxes and delivering the valentines. Girls dropped theirs through the slits with great flare. The boys acted embarrassed as they jammed in their valentines.

Miss Mitchell covered her old brown desk with a red tablecloth. Lemonade and pink frosted cupcakes magically appeared. At last it was time to look at our valentines. The classroom echoed with sounds of ripping envelopes. High-pitched "ohhhs" and "ahhhs" came from the girls. Boys shyly cleared their throats with big gulps of lemonade.

Miss Mitchell's seventh-grade class at Margaret Park Grade School, Akron, Ohio, in 1942. I am the second girl from the left in the fourth row from the front. Eddie is the sixth boy from the left in the row in front of me.

I opened up a cute one from my teacher. The next several were silly valentines from my best girlfriends. Then I opened three in a row, all from the same person. When I quickly glanced in his direction, his face said it all!

I could hardly wait to tell my two best friends that Eddie liked me. And I liked him, too! I watched as he opened the bright red envelope with a bit of a romantic, lacy card inside. His face lit up. We smiled across two rows of desks. Cupid finally delivered! ❖

Valentine Box Supper

By Betty Thomason

The Mazeland School in Runnels County, which I attended, held an annual Valentine's Day box supper. The Feb. 14, 1939, event especially stands out in my memory. A week before the event, Mama found a clean cardboard carton at the grocery store. "This will be the right size to pack our box meal," she said.

I was a month shy of my eighth birthday, and Mama agreed to let me decorate the empty box. "Make the decorations appealing so someone will bid a high price for what we contribute," she said. "We want our box of goodies to bring in money for your school."

Someone had decorated a doll buggy instead of a box.

Staring at that plain brown carton, I was stumped. "How do I decorate this box?"

"What are you mumbling about?" Mama asked. "Decorate with paper."

Then Mama helped speed the process along by making a thin paste of flour and water: a little flour, a little water, heat on the stove, stir like mad and set aside to cool. She always got the proportions just right. (I can make that paste, too, but my recipe is always trial-and-error.)

As soon as the paste cooled, Mama cut brown paper bags the right size to cover the box. She helped me glue the pieces to the sides and fold the edges over the inside of the container and paste them down. I held the edges until they were nearly dry to make sure they stuck.

Then I started the actual decorating by cutting out different sizes of paper hearts from red construction paper. Using a crayon, I wrote little valentine sentiments like "I love you" and "You are my Valentine" on the hearts. Then I glued the paper hearts all over the sides and top of the box and left the box to dry.

On the day of the box supper, I enlisted Mama's aid to fill the box. In summertime she sometimes packed a lunch of fried chicken, potato salad, fresh tomatoes and cucumbers. But this was February. We had some fresh homemade sausage, so Mama made a pan of biscuits and fried sausage patties. The aroma filled the kitchen, and the smoke from the frying pan gave the air a pleasant, warm haze. When the food was ready, Mama made six sausage-and-biscuit sandwiches for the box. I couldn't think of anyone who wouldn't love to eat Mama's delicious biscuits and sausages at that box supper.

Mama told me to stack four paper plates over the bottom of the box. I lined up the sandwiches on the paper plates, covered them with a napkin and placed four hard-boiled eggs to one side of the paper plates per Mama's instructions. On the other side of the biscuits—the crowning glory—Mama placed a big section of layered chocolate cake. She had made it early in the day with my help and iced it with homemade fudge icing.

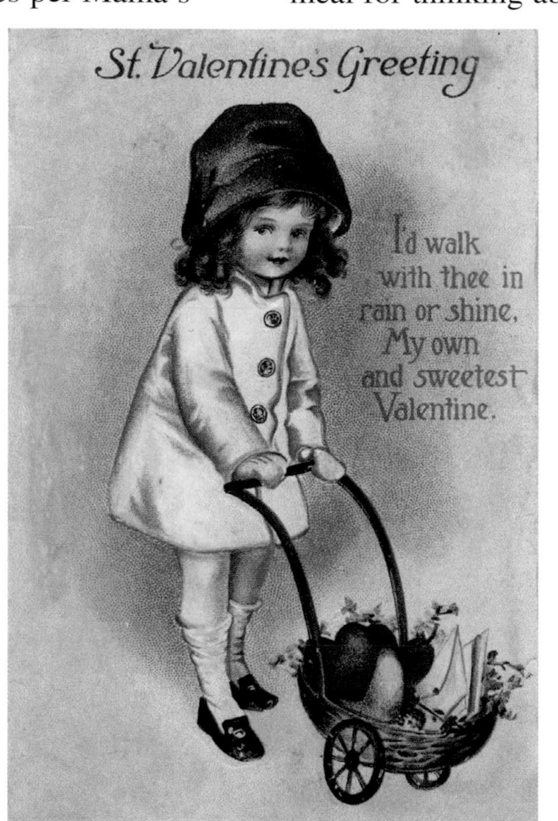

St. Valentine's Greeting
I'd walk with thee in rain or shine, My own and sweetest Valentine.

Mama saved half the cake for our family. "Half a cake will feed a family of five or six anyway," she said, wiping cake crumbs from the cutting board.

In the past, some of the box suppers Dad had purchased had lacked dessert and left us wishing for more to eat. This time, Mama made sure we would have dessert waiting for us when we returned home. I couldn't wait to get back to sink my teeth into that cake with the melt-in-your-mouth fudge icing.

At last we were ready for the evening's festivities. Dad, who was one of the school trustees, drove Mama, Gene, my 12-year-old brother, and me the half-mile to the school. My older brother, J.O., had already married and lived with his wife on another farm. And my third brother, Bud, was at McMurry College in Abilene, about 50 miles away. Our family had shrunk considerably.

When we arrived at the school for the box supper, I spotted the box I wanted Dad to bid on. Tugging on his shirtsleeve, I begged, "Dad, please, buy the one in the doll buggy?" Someone had decorated a doll buggy instead of a box. How appealing, especially to a little girl! I had never owned a doll buggy before—only a homemade doll bed.

Finally the auctioneer held up the doll buggy with the food inside. Dad started the bidding and finally outbid everyone else. The buggy belonged to me! I thought. How thrilled I was when Dad wheeled the doll buggy over to our place at the table. I could hardly eat my meal for thinking about taking the buggy home with me. Recalling the scant amount of food that buggy contained, I am sure Dad paid too much to buy it for me.

Actually, I don't remember what we ate, but I do know visions of Mama's chocolate cake waiting for us at home kept popping into my head.

But all my happy visions disappeared just as quickly when the buggy's owners came around to our table. Of all things, they asked Dad to return the buggy after the meal! I couldn't watch; I felt too let down. I wondered why he didn't put up an argument, but he didn't.

Mama took me aside and said, "We have to forgive people who sometimes disappoint us."

"Even people who tempt little girls with a doll buggy?" I asked. But I managed to stifle my hurt emotions for the moment.

To cheer me up, many neighbors came around to our table. They commented on how prettily I had decorated the box we brought. They told me the printed "I Love You" messages touched their hearts. The person who bought our box bragged on Mama's biscuits, sausage and chocolate cake.

The chocolate cake! I had forgotten all about it. I *did* have something to look forward to after all: a big piece of my favorite chocolate cake when we got home.

Despite everything, it was a good Valentine's Day box supper because people who cared offered me kind comments when they knew I needed them most. The attention made me feel better—that and the fact that Mama's chocolate cake was waiting for us at home. ❖

A Special Easter

By Mary L. Krull

The Easter season means different things to many people. To some people it signifies a time of spiritual renewal, and to others a time for family reunions and festive dinners. To many young children it brings thoughts of the Easter bunny, egg hunts and colorful baskets filled with sugary treats, and a visit to Grandmother's house.

During the 1940s when our country was at war, sugar and butter were rationed for the war effort. Homemade candy and frosted cakes were rare treats for many people.

For several days before Easter and the spring school recess, our first-grade teacher—I'll call her Miss Perkins—set aside some time each day to teach the children how to make little Easter baskets from colorful construction paper.

She taught us how to measure and carefully cut the notches in the paper at the proper places, and then fold it into a basket.

Our first-grade teacher taught us how to make little Easter baskets.

Each of the corners was glued together before a paper handle was attached. Grass for the basket was made by cutting green paper into tiny, narrow strips.

We were instructed to place our baskets on our desks next to the inkwell. Later on, before we were dismissed for the spring recess, the Easter Bunny would come and fill each basket with candy eggs and chocolate bunnies.

It seemed unusually cold and damp that spring when I attended first grade at Theodore Roosevelt School. While my classmates were busy every day creating their colorful little baskets, I was recovering at home from a cold and the measles, and could not be there to finish my paper basket. By the time I returned to school, it was only a day or two before the start of the Easter recess.

I had forgotten about the Easter basket project until I entered the classroom the morning I returned to school. I wanted to finish my little basket, but Miss Perkins insisted that there was no time for that. There were lessons to learn, and we had work to do.

Near the close of the school day, Miss Perkins went to the storage closet in the classroom. She brought a large shopping bag to her desk and carefully removed several bags of candy eggs, chocolate bunnies and other candies. The children *"oohed"* and *"aahed"* as they watched in eager anticipation.

All eyes focused on Miss Perkins as she walked between the aisles, placing handfuls of candy in each basket. As she filled each basket, the children would respond with a grateful "Thank you, Miss Perkins!"

Hoping that I would get some candy too, I placed a sheet of lined tablet paper on my desk next to the inkwell as a substitute for my unfinished paper basket. As Miss Perkins approached my desk, I wondered if she would give me some candy too.

But Miss Perkins walked past my desk. She noticed the sheet of tablet paper on my desk, but announced, "Anyone without their paper basket will not get any candy!"

My heart sank. I could not help it that I had been sick at home when everyone else was busy at school making Easter baskets. But Miss Perkins was adamant about her rules. No basket, no candy. I could feel my cheeks grow red and warm from embarrassment as all of the other children turned and looked at me.

I was the only one in the class who missed school and did not have a paper Easter basket. As my chin sank lower and lower, my head bowed. I hoped that no one would notice the tears I fought back.

As soon as the last basket was filled, Miss Perkins returned to her desk at the front of the room. There she carefully folded the tops of the bags of candy before returning them to the shelf in the closet.

Before she could return the bags of candy to the storage closet shelf and close the door, each of the girls and boys slipped very quietly from their seats, two and three at a time, to place a piece or two of their candy on my sheet of paper. The teacher noticed, but said nothing.

Now I had some candy, too! But best of all, I had some new friends that first year of school. They were special friends, too, because they shared more than just their candy with me that Easter season.

The compassion and caring shown to me by the other children in that first year of school made a lasting impression on me. Their generosity was a lesson that I used to teach my own son when he entered first grade.

After so many years, I cannot remember my classmates' names, but I will never forget their smiling faces and generosity from those long-ago Good Old Days. ❖

"May all
your clouds
be swept
away
To leave a
Glorious
Easter Day.

Easter Bouquet

By Letha Fuller

Bluebells rang the message:
"This is Easter Day.
Come to service, little friends,
Dress in bright array."

Lilies beamed in cream and white,
Tulips came in red;
Jonquil wore a yellow dress,
And hat upon her head.

Iris came in purple.
Narcissus, we are told,
Looked lovely in her frills of white
With her crown of gold.

Fragrant little hyacinths
Appeared in lilac, pink and rose,
But Jack-in-the-pulpit
Wore very somber clothes.

What a congregation!
A very sweet bouquet
Came to celebrate
That happy Easter Day.

May Day Frolics

By Lucinda Strine

Do you remember the Maypole dances we performed in days of yore? I think it took 16 girls, each controlling a long pastel streamer, to complete the complicated weaving. Half the girls traipsed one direction in and out, while the other bunch met them going around the other way, making a colorful design at the top. This was the tradition of longstanding for our "Last Day of School" celebration at Ruggles-Troy High in Nova, Ashland County, Ohio, in the 1940s. We girls practiced in gym class for at least a month prior to the big day.

The sophomore and junior girls performed the festive dance. If it rained, this entertainment was held in the stuffy, crowded gym. Our school wasn't the only one to celebrate this way. Hubby remembers a May Day celebration, too, on May 1 in their country high school.

The second year I was to dance around the pole, a few girls decided it would be better if we all wore matching dresses. They picked out a certain dress with pastel flowers from the Spiegel catalog. It cost $2.98 plus shipping! That was a large expenditure for nonessentials for our farm family back in the 1940s. That was also the year I turned my ankle while practicing. I skipped around painfully, but I refused to let it force me to quit. That pain I still remember!

The queen was adorned in a long gown of white satin with a train.

The special dress arrived. It was not nearly as pretty as pictured. It was flimsy, cheap cotton that had to be starched after each wearing or it would "look like a dishrag," as Mom was fond of saying. Only three other girls actually had ordered a similar one.

I'd like to think that that was the last of my battles with teen peer pressure, at least about clothes. Alas, it wasn't!

For the next year's ceremony for crowning the Queen of May, we senior girls all needed a new dress—and this time it was to be formal! The queen was chosen, and all seven of her classmates were attendants who were expected to wear long pastel gowns, complete with corsages, and carry a maroon peony. I still have a picture of us all in a row, formally gowned, in front of the old school building (which since has been torn down).

The queen was adorned in a long gown of white satin with a train, much like a bride's. She carried a bouquet of fresh flowers. A blond beauty she was! This procession marched to the throne to the music of the *Grand March* from *Aida.* Over the years I grew to love this triumphant refrain so much that I planned to use it for my own wedding march someday. (I didn't.)

Above: I am shown in my formal with my new graduation watch, holding a wine peony and wearing the necklace I was awarded for being class salutatorian. Below: The seven girls in the May Queen's court in May 1946. I am at the far right. The blonde with white flowers near the center is the queen.

After the winding of the pole, there were other musical numbers to enjoy after the queen and her court were seated. Perhaps it was the music teacher who helped oversee the proceedings; we were told very emphatically that the regular classroom faculty were much too busy completing final reports to join the frivolity.

The fish fry that followed was out of this world. Townspeople caught the fish in Lake Erie and cooked them in hot oil in a huge, drumlike apparatus.

They labored over this bubbling, steamy "stove" most of the day. Though there was also a potluck dinner at noon, I only remember the unspeakably delectable taste of deep-fried fish—the high point of the day for me!

One year the strawberries were beginning to ripen on the last Friday in May, adding to the bountiful feast. This was all too good to be confined to a single day, of course.

The crowning of the Queen of May fired the imagination of my two sisters and me. As youngsters, after watching this drama year after year, we would dress up and play "May Queen" far into June. By then the light blue iris were blooming in abundance for a queen's bouquet.

As older sister, I always wanted to be May Queen, but just as often I was outvoted by younger sisters to take turns.

Our favorite costume was a couple of discarded lace curtains to drape around us for a white formal with a train.

We marched from the front porch to the back steps where the crowning took place. Was the crown made of yellow dandelions intertwined? That detail escapes me.

But I do remember that if we didn't all three keep in time with the "hesitation step," we had to start all over!

Like many other local happenings in the country schools, these events have gone by the wayside. But what a joyous time it was!

Do you remember? ❖

Decoration Day 1933

By Betty Wallace Scott

In front of the blackboard, facing the classroom door, we were lined up by height, two abreast. Every other couple were the lucky ones who shouldered the child-size, 48-star American flags.

Teacher marshaled us down the stairs to the school yard. "Quiet! Keep in place!" From youngest to oldest, the classes fell into order in the middle of the brick street. Following the school band, we paraded past dads under straw hats, mothers in print dresses, grandpas with canes and tykes in carriages.

Fourth of July Parade by Jay Killian, House of White Birches nostalgia archives

The May sun grew hot and our legs ached from the long walk to Grandview Cemetery, but we stood respectfully for the Pledge of Allegiance and the oration beside the war memorial.

A line of World War veterans lifted their rifles to fire into the blue sky, saluting those who had died for country and God. We covered our ears and scrunched our eyes against the volleys.

Released from custody, we straggled back to the schoolhouse to get our report cards, sigh in relief that we had been passed to the next grade, and say goodbye to the teacher and the schoolroom.

Then we jumped joyfully into the freedom of summer, not even realizing how blessed we were to be growing up in an America that still revered Decoration Day. ❖

What About Billy?

By Agnes Reedy-Mayne

Whenever April frolics into May, my thoughts turn back to the May Day festivities I enjoyed years ago. No doubt you have your own cherished memories. May I share one of mine? In 1936, I was a new teacher at Myrtle Grove School in Myrtle Grove, a suburb of Pensacola, Fla. The faculty was enthusiastically launching into several new projects, including a gala May Day program. The principal agreed, with the stipulation that every child would have a part. With around 200 pupils in grades one through eight, there was a lot of planning to do.

Plans were made and laid several months ahead. The May queen and king would be chosen from the seventh- and eighth-grade pupils. Fifth- and sixth-graders would sing a medley of spring songs. Third- and fourth-graders would have the maypole dance; as their teacher, I was in charge of this. And pupils in the first and second grades would be flower fairies. A boy and a girl from each classroom would be selected as maids and knights, members of the royal court. The big boys (seventh- and eighth-graders) erected a stage in the large schoolyard where the royal court would sit.

When choosing partners for the Maypole dance, nobody wanted Billy.

Everything progressed nicely except for one problem: Where would Billy fit in?

Billy, in my fourth-grade class, was bigger and several years older than the others. (Social promotion was several years in the future.) Fat and clumsy, he wore a habitual scowl. He often skipped school until the truant officer threatened to get the law after his parents. When choosing partners for the maypole dance, nobody wanted Billy.

"Maybe he could sing with us," the fifth- and sixth-grade teachers offered hopefully. But Billy would not sing.

"Maybe he would like to help the other pupils," someone suggested. Those children were proudly arranging and rearranging the stage decorations. But Billy refused to participate.

Several times I approached the principal, who also taught the seventh and eighth grades. "What about Billy?" I'd ask.

"Find a place for him," she'd invariably insist. Busy with so many details, I still had Billy on my mind. What could he do?

What about a maypole? I was wondering. Mr. Dave had the answer. Mr. Dave was our indispensable janitor and a friend to all. "I'll get you one," he said, "but you'll have to practice on something else because I won't be able to get this to the school until the day of the program."

That satisfied us. We practiced with makeshift streamers on a pole from Amy's mother's clothesline. Billy watched sullenly.

Finally, the great day came. Our program was scheduled to begin at 2 p.m. Such a hubbub of last-minute preparations!

But, "Where is Mr. Dave?" I fretted.

"He said he'd be here at noon," the principal answered, adjusting a cape on a first-grade boy. "That'll give you time to decorate the top and all."

Mr. Dave finally arrived, bringing a tall pole in a truck. He propped it against the back of the truck and proudly showed us how he had rigged a small wheel to the top. The girls decorated the wheel with garlands of flowers and fastened to it the 18 pink and blue streamers that Annie's mother had made from crisp cotton fabric. At the bottom of the pole, four heavy planks were nailed crosswise to support it. Then Mr. Dave and the big boys carried it to its designated place and stood it upright.

The medley of spring songs had ended, and it was time for the maypole dance. Eighteen children took their places, streamers in hand. But before the music started, everyone gasped in dismay. The maypole was leaning! One of the planks at the base was evidently smaller and weaker than the others.

My heart sank. What could we do? There was no time to find more support.

Suddenly I felt a hand on my shoulder and heard a boy's voice say, "Teacher, I can fix it." With that, Billy crouched on the offending plank, and his weight adjusted the balance. The day was saved. Billy became a hero among the other students, and thereafter took his rightful place among them. ❖

Miss Reedy's fourth-grade class at Myrtle Grove School, 1937, May Day program.

AMERICAN

My Last Day of School

By George Drianis

OOOOOH! Remember the times that your parents told you about walking to school and all the hardships endured along the way? I know I've told those stories over and over again until our son would say: "Yes, Dad, I know—through five feet of snow for miles and miles, breath-taking wind, howling wolves and …" Well, you get the drift of it.

One such conversation brought back a memory of a spring day—the last day of school in 1939 in the small town of Ray, Minnesota, just south of International Falls. I was nine years old and just completing the fifth grade.

We had just moved into a new brick schoolhouse that had been built by the Public Works Administration. The classrooms were much nicer even though there were still only three classrooms for all eight grades.

I was nine years old and just completing the fifth grade.

Grades one and two were in one room, grades three, four and five in the next and grades six, seven and eight in the third.

Each room had one teacher who taught all subjects for all grades in that room. This was sometimes very distracting since one grade was being instructed in perhaps history while the other students in other grades were trying to concentrate on geography or arithmetic. Sometimes we paid more attention to the subject being taught rather than our own studies. The class size was determined by the number of kids of school age in the township and not by a teacher-student ratio. When students completed the eighth grade, they were bussed to International Falls each morning and returned in the evening.

All the desks were new and of the same model, and they could be adjusted so your feet would rest on the floor instead of dangling if your legs were too short. We now had electric lights and a drinking fountain that did not require refilling by the janitor after she carried it from the hand-pumped well down the hill. Surely not least, we had an indoor toilet at long last. An indoor toilet in northern Minnesota winters is surely no luxury, remembering how we bundled up to go to the toilet down the hill from the old school building.

Now comes the "second course" from our son: "Yes, I know: 'Six feet of snow, wind and wolves howling, 40 degrees below zero, only a thin coat to block the wind and …" Well, you get the drift of it.

Facing page: September 1955 *Wee Wisdom* magazine, House of White Birches nostalgia archives

I don't know why I would have taken my arithmetic book home the previous night, but I didn't have it to turn in when the teacher called my name. Before handing books in to store for the summer, we had to erase all our marks (and of course the previous kid's marks that hadn't been erased) and then lick and paste onionskin over any tears in the pages.

So while all the other kids could let their minds drift into thoughts of summer, mine was preoccupied with the immediate problem.

When my teacher called my name, I told her that I had forgotten my book at home. "Go get it," she said. I thought this was unusual, but in the old days no kid spoke back to a teacher. I left the schoolhouse at about 9 a.m.

Six feet of snow, wind and wolves howling, 40 degrees below zero.

About one-half mile from the school, I heard a car approaching from the rear and I got off the road and waited for it to reach me, thinking that I would get a ride. That was short-lived, because the driver honked, waved, smiled, passed and left me standing in the dust. I don't know why he smiled. Perhaps just being neighborly.

Eventually I reached our farm. My mother was very surprised to see me because no one was ever expected home before early evening. She was washing clothes and asked what was wrong since I was home at noon on a school day. I told her I had forgotten my math book that morning, and the teacher had sent me to get it. She looked very concerned. I asked what I could have to eat, but since she was washing clothes, nothing was prepared.

After taking off my shoes and socks to ease the discomfort of a blister on a heel, I headed out the door eating a catsup sandwich. Everything, including plain catsup, tasted good on homemade bread.

The blister on my heel was probably caused by a hole in my sock, rather than a shoe too large for me. It was the end of the school year and our school clothes, purchased nine months before, were just beginning to fit right. During the Great Depression, we always had to "grow into" new clothes, and by the time that happened, they were nearly worn out. The extra length also gave material for patches. Most of us had only two school outfits and changed on Monday mornings. Bib overalls was the normal school attire for most boys. A pair of shoes usually lasted a little longer since we wore rubber boots in the winter. Boots could always be made to fit with one more (or less) pair of socks. It was suggested that we wear shoes with overshoes if we had them because wearing rubber boots indoors all day was bad for our eyes. This must have been true, since I had to get reading glasses at age 63.

I arrived back at the school just as the last period was about to begin. After getting a drink of water, I went in and gave my book to the teacher.

Immediately I was given a stern lecture. "I told you to go home, get your book and here you are, gone all day, nothing done, bare-footed and soon it will be time to go home!"

"I couldn't make it any faster," I said quietly and apologetically to the teacher. "It was eleven miles."

Was she surprised! I sensed that she felt awful! "I thought you lived in town," she said, this time much more calmly. "Why didn't you say something?"

I wondered if she had noticed that I was walking on the ball of my foot. The five and one-half miles back probably would have been easier with my shoes on. The blister was low on the heel, and the gravel road had only made it worse. The cool linoleum tiles felt good on my bare feet.

I hurried to clear the last things from my desk. I glanced up once and saw the teacher looking at me. Her eyes and smile pleaded for understanding. They seemed to say: "I want you to know that I am truly sorry … forgive me for …"

It's too bad that I had graduated to the third room of that little country school. I think there was a good chance that she wanted to make it all up to me when school resumed in the fall.

I wouldn't have wanted to disappoint her, discourage her efforts, or … well, you get the drift of it. ❖

Her Best Thanksgiving

By Faye B. Hughes

When Aunt Garnet was a girl, the teachers at her one-room country school offered a prize each Thanksgiving to the child who wrote the most interesting story about their Thanksgiving Day.

A boy would receive a little pocketknife, and a girl, a bottle of Blue Waltz perfume.

Aunt Garnet was 12, and she had never had a bottle of perfume. How she coveted it!

Grandpa, Aunt Garnet's father, was an evangelist, and he was often away from home two or three weeks at a time. Such was the case this particular Thanksgiving week.

Money was very scarce, so Grandma and the children would be staying home and having soup beans and homemade bread for their Thanksgiving dinner.

Garnet was sure that there was nothing in her Thanksgiving to write about, but she still dreamed of owning that perfume. But how? At last she got an idea, and she sat down to write. She wrote that her father was home for the holiday, and her family rode in their sleigh to Grandpa Hundley's farm. (Aunt Garnet's family had no sleigh, but they did have a Grandpa Hundley who lived on a farm.)

In Aunt Garnet's story, all her aunts and uncles were there, and she had a wonderful time playing in the haymow with her cousins.

Grandma Hundley served a feast fit for a king, with turkey and all the trimmings, plus several kinds of pie for dessert. How wonderful everything tasted! And after dinner, the cousins returned to the haymow for more games.

Later, they all went outside and built a snowman and a snow fort. They divided up into teams and had a marvelous snowball fight. The day passed all too soon, and at dusk, Aunt Garnet and her family got back into their sleigh and returned home, having enjoyed a perfect Thanksgiving Day.

When Aunt Garnet returned to school after the holiday, she turned in her story. The following day it was returned to her.

It was marked with the grade "A," and her teacher had added a note: "Very good." Aunt Garnet was thrilled when she won the bottle of perfume.

But back home, her mother was at a loss to understand. How could staying home and eating soup beans make for such an interesting story?

Later, she found Garnet's story, and she was horrified by all the lies Garnet had written. It was especially bad because Garnet was a minister's daughter and knew better. Aunt Garnet's mother told her not to open the perfume. Tomorrow, her mother said, she would go with Garnet to take it back and tell her teacher the truth.

Garnet cried all the way to school the next day. But her teacher saw things differently. Whether the story was true or not, the teacher said, Garnet had put a lot of effort into writing it.

Besides, her punctuation and spelling had been perfect—and it *was* very interesting. Garnet had earned the perfume, her teacher said, and should be allowed to keep it.

For many years thereafter, Aunt Garnet used Blue Waltz perfume and loved it. And she turned out to have a talent for fiction. When we were children, we loved to go to Aunt Garnet's house because she always entertained us each evening with wonderful stories.

So as it turned out, her Thanksgiving story was only her first masterpiece. ❖

Frederic Stanley

The Big Scare

By James D. Doggette Jr.

Halloween isn't just for the kids; it's also for the young at heart. It is no truer today than it was in New Orleans in 1950. I was going to an old Catholic school named Holy Trinity, about seven blocks from my house. The campus was huge. It encompassed an entire city block. Within its 10-foot stone walls were the cathedral, nunnery, schoolhouse, supply warehouse, courtyard, play yard, and assorted staff buildings.

With Halloween fast approaching, the nuns got together with the mothers and decided to have a special party for the kids. Money donations poured in. Mothers and fathers also donated their time and talents. Moms baked all sorts of cookies, cupcakes and cakes. Dads built a mockup of a haunted mansion with accompanying graveyard in the far corner of the warehouse. The nuns set up tables and chairs, then devised a program.

Finally, everything was ready. When the big night came, we were ushered in to view the kaleidoscopic panorama. It was a child's dream. Decorations hung everywhere, complete with smiling jack-o'-lanterns and cobwebs. Ghosts, witches, goblins and ghouls lurked in every corner. Crepe-paper spiders hung from the ceilings along with bats and owls.

The lush tables were filled with all kinds of Halloween candies and treats. Each child received a papier-mâché jack-o'-lantern filled with suckers, candy corn, licorice and other delightful goodies.

We played games like "Button, Button, Who's Got the Button?" and bobbed for apples. Prizes were given to the winners. We even had a cake walk.

Soon the time came for the master of ceremonies. Everyone took their seats and the lights were lowered. Low-key lights were trained on the haunted house. The scene was completed with spooky sound effects, background music, and pots of water with dry ice in them, which made a peculiar fog arise from the graveyard.

The storyteller wove a macabre tale about a mad scientist, who lived alone in the mansion, and the disappearance of local folks. The psychotic doctor operated on his unfortunate patients and passed out the body parts for all to feel: cooked pasta noodles for veins, large peeled grapes for eyeballs, peeled, soggy eggplant for a stomach, etc.

The momentum built into a crescendo and mass hysteria took over. Then the emcee announced that the doctor's next patient would be—"YOOOU!"

With that, nuns dressed as hobgoblins burst through the crepe-paper windows of the old haunted mansion. They ran to grab students and mothers. Everyone began screaming.

The lights came back up to normal. The master of ceremonies reassured everyone, and then introduced his helpers and staff, one by one.

About that time, we heard loud, sharp knocks on both of the large wooden doors to the warehouse. When the doors were opened to admit these late-arriving guests, in walked four police officers of the Fifth District, billy clubs in hand.

Mother Superior walked over to them and addressed an elderly officer wearing sergeant's stripes. He said they had had a call about someone being murdered or something over at Holy Trinity. He looked around at the students, mothers, decorations and costumes, and then began laughing. "I can see there's no problem here," he chuckled. The officer bid us good night and tipped his hat. Then the policemen left.

It seems that that special Halloween was a memorable one for many more people than had been planned! ❖

JOHN FALTER

School Gift Exchange

By Glen Herndon

Early in December 1935, when I was in second grade, Mrs. Brewer, our teacher, had us write our names on slips of paper and drop them into a shoe box. We were going to have a class Christmas gift exchange again.

She was well aware that many of our families were nearly destitute. We lived in the scrub oak country of the oil fields of Oklahoma, near Seminole, but the oil boom was long since over and many of our daddies were working for as little as a dollar a day. So she said no one had to buy anything; we could bring something homemade. But if we did buy our gift for the exchange, it was not to cost more than 25 cents.

We were a combined class of first- and second-graders, and there were about 38 of us. Earlier, Teacher had brought in a little tree and set it up on a big table up in front of the room, and then we all made decorations for it. It was not our custom to put up a tree at home, so I really enjoyed the bright colors of all the doodads and strings of popcorn and colored paper chains.

My heart pounded. To hear him tell it, he already had everything.

When I reached into the shoe box and withdrew Bill Brady's name, my heart pounded. He was a rich kid. To hear him tell it, he already had everything. We didn't doubt it, because for show-and-tell he was apt to bring in some of his expensive toys. His folks had a car deliver him to school and pick him up every afternoon, and he wore suits a lot. The rest of us just wore bib overalls. He didn't mix in with us boys, and at recess he would mostly hang around the swings, saying he didn't want to get dirty on the red playground soil. Though Teacher tried to help us all learn to be tolerant, he was pretty easy to dislike.

At home, Mother said she would give me a quarter from her egg money for a gift for him. On the next trip to town, I picked out a neat little cast-metal cannon that shot a single BB when you pulled a plunger at the base of the barrel. The dime store had a lot of selections, but Mother agreed that he'd like the cannon. It was a gift I would have liked to get myself, and I wanted to try it out. But Mother let me shoot only one BB to make sure it worked before she wrapped it so that I wouldn't be tempted to use it and break it.

After a very long wait, the gift exchange day finally arrived. Teacher had little brown bags of hard candies for us all. Many of the gifts were homemade. There was a neat slingshot made from the fork of a sapling tree, a hand-carved yo-yo, and a whistle made from a little piece of sapling branch. There were a number of pieces of

Facing page: *Classroom Christmas* by John Falter © 1951 SEPS: Licensed by Curtis Publishing

needlework, embroidery on flour-sack towels, and cookies, gingerbread men, popcorn balls, homemade fudge and taffy.

Bill Brady unwrapped his cannon, and I watched as a big smile lit his eyes behind his little, round, steel-rimmed glasses. He looked over at me and yelled, "Thanks!" Then he loaded his cannon and shot one BB at the blackboard. Ping! Wouldn't you know it? It bounced back and hit Teacher's glasses! She took them off immediately to see if the lens was damaged. It wasn't, but she took the cannon forcefully from Bill and put it in her desk drawer. He could take it home, but he couldn't use it at the party any more.

I heard him say he could hardly wait to get the cannon home so he could shoot at his lead soldiers. But secretly, I smiled a little inside that he had gotten into a little trouble with Teacher.

My gift was from a redheaded, freckle-faced boy with sparkling blue eyes and a ready smile—good ol' Sam. He was the best-liked boy in our class because of his nature, and I sat with him a lot to help him get his lessons. Sam lived with his widowed dad in a fishing shanty somewhere down by the river, and I don't know if he ever got a bath, or if they washed many clothes. He generally had a certain aura about his person.

I unwrapped my gift, which was done up in a small brown bag with a string tied around it. It was a ceramic Indian chief bank, complete with war bonnet and fierce look. Gosh, it was neat! Where could he have gotten it? "Shake it," Sam said. "Dad put a dime in it so's you'll never be broke!"

Then I got to see his present. Someone had gotten him a little compass, and he allowed that he would never get lost on the river or in the woods.

When I got home, Dad gave me a lecture about how now, with the bank, I could save money.

But I never got any, so how could I save any?

As I got older, I did odd jobs and some menial things. I tried to stash my coins in the bank, but something always came along for me to spend my savings on. My older brother, Herbert, showed me how to run a table knife into the slot and coax the coins out without having to break the bank.

My family moved a number of times; we even migrated to California. Eventually I lost track of my wonderful bank that always brought such happy memories of that gift exchange.

And I never took the dime out—or if I did, I put it back so I would never be broke! I've often wondered if the person finding it could fathom the significance of the dime and leave it there. ❖

The Spirit of Christmas

By Audrey Corn

Teacher was strict, but she was nice, and we liked her. In early December, she let us vote. "How many of you want a grab bag at the Christmas party?" Teacher asked. Every hand in the room shot up.

"There will be some rules," Teacher warned. I lived in Brooklyn, N.Y., in the 1940s. Back then, kids were used to rules.

Teacher explained the plan. She would write each of our names on a separate piece of paper, then put the papers in a shoebox. We would close our eyes and draw a name. "Think of yourselves as Secret Santas!" Teacher said. "You can't tell anyone the name you draw. You can't trade names. And you can't spend more than 25 cents."

Some of our parents couldn't afford 25 cents, so Teacher made one more rule. "You can spend less than 25 cents, or make your gift," she added. Teacher forgot to include special instructions for kids (like me) who drew their own names. Twenty-five cents to buy anything I wanted! Hot diggety dog!—and to heck with my guilty conscience.

For the next two weeks, I visited the five-and-dime every chance I got. There were dozens of treasures to choose from. Most cost 25 cents or less. I particularly liked a box of pink writing paper.

But when it came time to make my purchase, I discovered that it was no fun to buy my own gift and, day after day, I returned home empty-handed.

In the meantime, my classmates began to bring in mysterious bundles done up in colorful paper. Teacher put their packages in the big cloth sack near her desk.

Pretty soon, every kid except Timothy Matthiesen and me had brought in a present. Timmy was out sick with the measles. On Dec. 23, his brother stopped by with a package. That left me.

I had one day till the party. I decided to make a final trip to Woolworth's. Fun or no fun, I would buy myself the pink writing paper.

Mama noticed my long face. "What's eating you, child?" she asked.

I hadn't meant to blab, but the words came tumbling out. I told Mama how I'd drawn my own name, how I'd liked the idea that I could get anything I wanted.

"I should have told Teacher. It's no fun to buy my own presesnt. And I'll be the only kid without a surprise," I sobbed.

Mama was silent, mulling over my problem. If anyone could help me, it was Mama. Finally, she spoke. "Create your fun! You still have your quarter, don't you?"

"Yes, Mama."

"Good! Here's what we'll do," Mama said.

Our Christmas party started right after lunch. I'd bought my own gift, but I was as excited as anyone else. When Teacher called my name, I hurried to the front of the room to accept my package. I tore off the wrapping. "Tootsie Rolls!" I cried. "A big bag of Tootsie Rolls!"

The other kids had taken their gifts back to their desks. But not me! I stayed in the front of the room. "I have too many Tootsie Rolls to eat by myself. Can—I mean, *may*—I pass them out to the class?" I asked.

Teacher gave me a suspicious look. But the spirit of Christmas was in the air. "I'll let you share if you promise to save one for me!" Teacher joked.

I had asked the saleslady at Woolworth's to count out 25 penny-candy Tootsie Rolls. Now all of us, including Teacher, sucked our Tootsie Rolls slowly to make them last. And we "oohed" and "aahed' over our 25-cents-or-less grab-bag gifts. And I didn't miss my pink stationery one bit!

Wasn't the spirit of Christmas lovely back in the Good Old Days? ❖

The Show Must Go On

By Donald McKinney

I lost the lead in the Christmas play. For a 10-year-old boy in a one-room country school, it was the saddest day of my life. Not for eight more years did my dream come true. In 1920 the Christmas play was the big event of the school year.

Two of the bigger boys were sent to the woods to cut a 15-foot tree for the schoolroom. The foot-pump organ was moved out of the corner to make room for the tree, and our teacher, Miss Harris, gave us time off to string cranberries and popcorn for decorations.

Miss Harris selected the cast for the Christmas play early in December. I wanted the leading part of Joseph so I could wear a long bathrobe and a beard and gray wig. But I was in bed for six days with the measles.

When I returned to school, Miss Harris said, "You are going to be prompter for the play. It is a very important part. You need to learn the lines."

I wanted the leading part of Joseph so I could wear a long bathrobe and a beard and gray wig. But I was in bed for six days with the measles.

How exciting it was to get ready for Christmas! All 15 of us had parts in the play. Mr. Lundy built a real stage in the front of the schoolroom. He strung a wire from wall to wall, and Miss Harris used sheets for stage curtains, fastening them with safety pins so the curtain could be pulled open and shut. Using newspaper, I cleaned the seven coal-oil (kerosene) lamps that were mounted in brackets around the schoolroom walls.

Ten inches of snow had fallen the night of the play, but long before curtain time, the back of the room was filled with parents. We had a live baby for our manger and two live sheep for the nativity scene. The boys put on their false beards long before play time.

Miss Harris was worried; it was only 20 minutes before curtain time, and Esther, who had a leading role as an angel, had not showed up.

Then, at about 15 minutes to 7, a sleigh pulled up to the schoolhouse door. Esther's father, his face hidden by his big cap and the collar of his coat, stamped into the schoolroom. "Where is Miss Harris? Where is Miss Harris?" he called.

Our teacher pushed the curtain aside and went out to see him. "'Taint good news I got for you," he said. "Don't know how to say

My thespian days—and my desire to be a star—didn't end in fourth grade. In the photograph above, I am seated in the front row, shown in my role as the lead in our senior play, It Happened in June, *in 1928, eight years after my role as an angel in the Christmas play at my one-room school.*

it. Esther has lost her voice. She can't come. Her throat was sore when she got home from school, and Mom put her to bed. She can't be in the play tonight."

We stood as quiet as mice when Miss Harris came back behind the curtain. We looked to her as our only hope. We had worked so hard on the play.

Miss Harris was blunt. "You heard him. Esther can't be in the play tonight. We have to call it off and send your parents home. Esther had a leading part as the angel, and we can't have the play without her."

Then, as she said her last words, her eyes turned to me. "No, we *don't* have to call off the play," she announced. "The play will go on. Donald knows all of Esther's lines and her song." She walked over to me and took my hands in hers. "You are going to be our angel. You can do it. I know you can."

For a 10-year-old boy, it was the saddest day in my life.

There was a long silence. Nobody dared question the wisdom and authority of Miss Harris.

"Ruth and Thelma, you help me. The play starts in 10 minutes, as planned."

But there was still a problem. Esther was in the sixth grade and weighed 85 pounds. Her mother had worked for days, making her white angel's dress, complete with a flapping set of wings and a halo that fastened to a wire that swayed above her head. The hem of her gown touched the floor.

Miss Harris assured me that angels certainly could be men and wear wings. She had seen pictures of them. And she said they wore gowns, not pants. But I wasn't satisfied. I weighed 110 pounds and I was a head taller than Esther.

By linking three safety pins together, Miss Harris fastened my dress in the back. "Now don't you dare turn around on the stage. Don't let the audience see the back," she said. When I looked at myself in the mirror, I was ready to turn and run home through the snow. My spindly legs extended a foot below the hem of my dress. But it was too late to run. Mary and Joseph were beside the cradle with the baby on the stage. The curtain opened, and it was my time to go on.

The room was in an uproar at the sight of me. The older boys in the audience shouted and whistled. I could not speak.

I thought only of a long-legged country boy trying to take the part of a sweet little girl, playing the part on an angel.

I looked for an escape. Then I looked right into the eyes of Miss Harris, who was hidden from the audience across the stage. She was wringing her hands and big tears were running down her face.

I won't let her down. I can't *let her down!* I said to myself. Then I spoke my first lines, loud and clear: "Fear not, for behold! I bring you good tidings of great joy, which shall be to all people. Here in this stable has been born a Savior, which is Christ, the Lord!"

The laughter stopped. There was not a sound in the audience. I continued: "Glory to God in the highest, and on earth, peace and good will toward men!" Forgetting my costume, I poured out the words of the glorious birth of Jesus Christ, the Savior of all mankind.

I was the star of the play, the lead, when I thought I had lost everything. It was what I said that was important to those parents in 1920, not how I looked. Only their faith made it possible for them to labor such long hours on their farms. And I never dreamed that eight years later, I would really have the lead in my senior class play. ❖

Black Bloomers & A White Christmas

By Selma McCarthy

It was snowing that week before Christmas in 1930. Lillian and I were covered with it when we reached school. We tried to brush it off our clothes and shoes before we entered, but we still left small puddles behind us as we climbed the 12 stairs to the great hall. We stopped to look at the big tree in the middle of the hall. The shiny icicles and bright lights made it the prettiest tree I had ever seen. It was so tall that it nearly reached the ceiling.

"Doesn't it smell good, Lillian?"

"Yes, it smells better than pencil shavings or new books!"

"It smells like my grandma's woods." I reached out to touch the tree, but then I remembered that kids weren't supposed to. I pulled back my hand.

Billy was a sentinel and I was a mechanical French doll.

We saw Mr. Welton, the janitor, starting downstairs, and I was afraid he was going to ring the 8:15 tardy bell. I pulled Lillian into our cloakroom so that we wouldn't be late. All the rest of the kids had gone to their rooms. We hung up our coats and hats and took our seats in Miss Wickwire's room.

"Good morning, boys and girls! Do you like the snow?"

"We love it!" we all shouted.

"So do I. It is very nice for Christmas, just a week away. Shall we sing a Christmas song after the Pledge of Allegiance?"

"Yes, Ma'am!"

"What shall we sing?" Miss Wickwire asked.

"*Away in a Manger*," Leroy Watts said.

"All right, children?"

"All right!" we answered. After the pledge, Miss Wickwire started the song, and we sang along. Sometimes she had to stop and tell us the next words, and then we would sing them.

"Very good for first-graders," Miss Wickwire told us. We were proud of our singing after she said that.

After recess was over, Marjean, Billy and I had to go to Miss Hartman's room to practice again for the Christmas play we were to be in that night at school. Miss Wickwire had chosen Marjean for the part of Raggedy Ann; Billy was a sentinel and I was a mechanical French doll.

Marjean was the prettiest girl in Tecumseh School, with shingle-bobbed blond hair and big blue eyes.

Her knee stockings were the envy of every girl in our room. We all had to wear long stockings, and I had to wear long underwear and black sateen bloomers, too. I had to lap the underwear legs over in the back, and they made lumps under my stockings. I was ashamed of those lumps. I wanted to wear knee stockings, too.

Billy was stuck on Marjean, and I was stuck on Billy. Drat! In the play, I had to be in a big box wrapped in white and tied with a red ribbon. Billy was supposed to stand by the box and untie the ribbon so I could get out when Miss Hartman stared to play Toyland on the piano.

When I got out, I had to move like a wind-up doll. All Marjean had to do was sit in a chair, cross her legs and roll her eyes at Billy when he "wound" me up. When Miss Hartman nodded to me, I was supposed to pretend I was run-down, then bend over and let my arms swing freely.

Everything was going well at rehearsal. Then a second-grade boy, Tom Talley, beat a hole in his drum by accident. Ruth Turner, from the third grade, fell over the toy train, and Billy whispered, "Your bloomers are showing!" when he rewound me.

I wondered if anyone else had seen. I looked at my "friend" sitting there with her legs crossed, and she snickered. Guess she had seen them, too. When we got back to our

February 1930 *Woman's World* magazine, House of White Birches nostalgia archives

room, Marjean raised her hand. Miss Wickwire nodded at her. "Miss Wickwire, during practice we saw Selma's black bloomers when she bent over," Marjean said. Everyone laughed and laughed. I could feel my face getting hot, and I wanted to run to the cloakroom and hide. Miss Wickwire came over to my desk.

"It's all right, honey. Those things happen to all of us sometimes." I felt better—I loved Miss Wickwire. The bell rang, and she dismissed us to go home.

"See you tonight, Selma. Do your best in the play!" Miss Wickwire said.

"I will," I answered as Lillian rushed up to me.

"Don't worry. It's OK. I wonder who Marjean thinks she is, telling Miss Wickwire that? She acts big because Billy likes her."

"I know she does," I sniffed. "She embarrassed me."

It was still snowing when we started home. By the time we got to Lillian's house, it was getting deep. Her mother told me that she and Mr. Reeves would come by in their car to get Mother and me at 6 o'clock. I thanked her and hurried home.

Mother had my favorite supper: vegetable soup! "Hurry, dear, and eat your supper, because I have to curl your hair for tonight. I pressed your costume, and it looks nice."

It is *pretty,* I decided as I looked at the red satin "doll" dress with underpants to match. I didn't have to wear my black bloomers or long underwear tonight—thank heaven!

Mother heated her curling iron in the chimney of the kerosene lamp and put my hair in curls all over my head. She put rouge on my cheeks and lips to make me look like a doll. I wondered how Marjean would look in her Raggedy Ann dress and the red Halloween wig Miss Hartman had given her to wear.

I was so excited to wear ankle socks—and no black bloomers—that I could hardly wait for the play to start. Back at school, Lillian nudged me as Marjean walked past in her costume and red wig. That wig was ugly! Lillian and I snickered.

At last Miss Hartman took us onstage behind the closed curtains and helped the kids find their places. Marjean missed her chair and landed on the floor. Her wig fell off, and she grabbed it off the floor and put it on backwards. Everyone laughed, and she was embarrassed. *Serves her right,* I thought.

I heard the curtains opening, and Billy opened my box when Miss Hartman played *Toyland.* I stepped out with mechanical movements, and the audience clapped for me. I was proud and happy.

When Billy rewound me, he whispered, "You sure look pretty without black bloomers!" My feet didn't seem to touch the floor after that. When I passed Marjean, I stuck out my tongue; she returned the favor. The audience laughed and threw Christmas candy kisses onstage for us.

When the play was over, Billy ignored Marjean and came over to me. He took me by the hand and led me from the stage to the cloakroom.

I was so excited that I could hardly wait to tell Lillian. I knew I just couldn't wear black bloomers again—especially since Billy liked me now.

"Mother," I began when she started toward me, "please don't *ever* make me wear those old black bloomers again. They just look awful, and Marjean Reel doesn't have to wear them!"

"Well, we'll discuss it in the morning. I am very proud of you. You really were very good in the play," she said.

"Thank you, Mother. I really tried to do my best. How did you like Marjean?"

"I thought she was cute, and I liked her performance, too."

Lillian came running up to us, beaming with excitement. "Selma, you were good!" She lowered her voice. "I can't say the same for Marjean." Loyal Lillian was saying just what I wanted to hear.

As we left the cloakroom arm in arm, I said to Lillian, "Guess what happened? Billy paid attention to me. I think he likes me!"

"Oh, I hope he does. Maybe we can outdo that Marjean yet!" We both tittered and went to stand in line for refreshments. It had been a wonderful night, and we were very happy. And there was a chance that I would never have to wear black bloomers again. ❖

Belles, Buddies & Bullies

Chapter Four

Like millions of others across this great North American continent, my life was molded by my experiences with belles, buddies and bullies in the schools of my Good Old Days.

Today's gangs are yesterday's bullies, and I learned how to handle a bully on the playground. James was our school bully, and he chose me to humiliate day after day until one fateful recess after Christmas. That was when he broke a toy car Santa had brought me—one of the few "store boughten" toys I received. Bully James found a hellion on his back and around his neck. He went screaming for the teacher, and I learned to never back down from a bully.

He went screaming for the teacher and I learned never to back down.

Affairs of the heart are the same generation to generation. Ours were just a lot more innocent then. I thought I had won Mary Lynn's affections when I chased only her in a game of freeze tag. Then came Valentine's Day. Mary Lynn didn't get me the big valentine I had seen at the general store. She didn't get me one of the little valentines in the package of 20. Heck, she didn't even draw me an arrow-pieced heart on a stupid piece of paper! That was how I learned to deal with rejection in the third grade.

Probably the most important life lesson I learned from my experiences in school, however, was the one about gambling. I had become a regular high roller by the time I was in fourth grade. First it was pitching pennies, then flipping nickels. But one day I made the mistake of playing marbles for "keepsies" with Sally.

I knew Sally was a good marble player, but she was a girl and no girl could beat me! She held an impressive bag of agates, but her shooter was what interested me. It was the best shooter I had ever seen. We made a bet: Whoever captured the most marbles from the ring drawn in the schoolyard dirt would win the other's shooter. It was a daring gamble for me; I had had my shooter for over a year, and it had never failed in the ring of competition.

Sally and I traded several pretty good runs, then I edged slightly into the lead about midway through the match. That's when the roof caved in. Sally punched out a good run of eight marbles or so and claimed a pretty good lead in marbles. I only got back four on my next round, while Sally pulled farther ahead with another good run. I did the math—I needed almost all of the last dozen marbles to keep from losing my shooter.

It was probably sweat poring off my forehead onto my shooting hand that caused the shooter to slip after just the third shot in my next round. Sally removed all suspense by smashing four agates from the ring for an insurmountable lead. I finished off what was left of the marbles and then begrudgingly handed Sally my shooter. Then and there I swore off gambling.

Those experiences of a lifetime are still with me. James taught me that most bullies are just cowards deep down. Mary Lynn—that hussy—helped me recognize true love when it came along in the form of my dear wife, Janice, a few years later. And, because of Sally, I have never had the temptation of playing the slots at Vegas or Reno. I learned from her to keep my money on the sure bets of life: God, family, good friends—love that lasts forever. Yes, I learned a lot in those school rooms back in the Good Old Days.

—Ken Tate

Hy Hintermeister

The Little Redheaded Girl

By Richard Blair

Life in 1940 was idyllic for a first-grader. The war wasn't far away of course, but I didn't know about such things yet, and so they were of no concern to me. Dad had a good job and there was enough money to go around, so we wanted for nothing. People still spoke to each other on the streets and left their houses unlocked, and the neighbor women still visited back and forth for coffee and gossip. Mothers were always home, and kids were expected to behave. A spanking still settled orneriness, and no one went to jail when one was administered.

I was attending first grade at Grant School in Cuyahoga Falls, Ohio, and my teacher was Mrs. Doakes. She was a wonderful elderly lady straight out of a Norman Rockwell painting. Mom and Dad were always there to care for, nurture and protect me. Life was good, very good.

Sometimes she got it all. When it came to candy, she was insatiable.

The one area where I was on my own was my love life. I was smitten at an early age. The object of my affection was a pretty little redheaded girl who giggled a lot and made my heart do flip-flops. She came to school about a month after classes began, and her name was Alice. All the other boys were taken with her, but I was the one who finally won her attention. Soon we were a couple. We hung out together at recess, and she would sit with me at lunchtime.

Lunchtime for me was a big deal, because in addition to my usual peanut butter sandwich, which I dearly loved, my mother would usually include a candy bar or maybe a cookie for dessert.

She always gave me a nickel to buy a half-pint of chocolate milk to wash it down with, as well. If I recall correctly, the milk sold at school cost only 3 cents, so that left me with an extra 2 cents in my pocket. Before I met Alice, the 2 cents would be spent at a little store on the way home to buy myself some candy; sometimes I managed to save my pennies until I had as much as a dime with which I might splurge and buy myself some little toy. On those occasions, I felt like Rockefeller himself.

But when I met Alice, all that changed. She would always ask for my candy bar or cookie, and of course I would give it to her. That was hard on me, but after all, what is love if it's not giving? I even

Facing page: *Carrying Her Books for Her* by Henry Hintermeister © 1937 SEPS: Licensed by Curtis Publishing

gave her half of my prized Popsicle stick collection, which I later learned she threw away.

Despite that, whatever I had was hers. Love is truly blind! For a couple of months, we continued our give-and-take romance—I would give and she would take.

Alice lived about four blocks from school in another direction from the route that I used. Nevertheless, I was soon walking her home every day after school. Along the way, we passed another little store that sold penny candy. Alice would go in with me, pick out the candy she liked, and I would buy it for her. I usually ate one little piece and gave her the rest. Sometimes she got it all. She was insatiable, when it came to candy.

I sulked along until we reached her house. By now the bag was empty, and so was my heart.

I noticed that she always had a few pennies of her own, and sometimes a nickel or dime as well, but she never spent her money. As long as I was paying for everything, she was only too happy to let me continue. When I could manage to save a little, I sometimes bought her a little toy, or maybe a coloring book as a special gift. I really felt like something on those occasions.

One time, I came down with the measles and had to stay away from school for a few weeks. I spent the whole time pining for Alice, afraid that she would forget me and take up with another boy. I had to suffer my worries by myself though, because this was not something a guy could talk over with his parents. Time seemed to drag, but eventually it was deemed safe to send me back to school.

On my return, I learned that Alice had dallied about a bit, but she did seem genuinely happy to see me again, and we were soon back as before. If anything had changed, it was only that her appetite had increased, and now, in addition to all the cookies and candy, she began expecting half of my peanut butter sandwich as well as a drink of my chocolate milk. Alice was becoming a little more difficult to support, and I was becoming hungry.

The day came when I refused to give her half of my sandwich, and she stomped away angrily. The next day, I coaxed her back by offering my whole lunch, and she took it. It was a poor gamble on my part, and I lost. The next day, she took it again. This continued for more than a week, and I was beginning to see Alice in a new light. Also, my pants were beginning to bag on me!

Then came that fateful day when we made our usual stop at the store for her candy. When the man handed me the little bag, I discovered that I had lost my pennies. I was flat broke! Without hesitation, Alice casually pulled out a dime of her own money and paid the man. My heart swelled with emotion, but alas, darker emotions were awaiting me outside. As we left the store, I walked along with her politely while waiting for her to open the bag and offer me the one piece I always ate.

The bag opened, her hand went in and then to her mouth. I still waited! She was chattering on and eating all the candy! At last, I had to ask for a piece, and when I did, she gave me a surprised look and explained that this was candy she had bought for herself. I could have my piece again tomorrow, when *I* bought it. So much for romance!

The farther I walked, the madder I got, but I said nothing. I sulked along until we reached her house. By now the bag was empty, and so was my heart.

On the walk home, I thought it over and decided that I didn't like Alice anymore. The next day, I pretended that nothing happened, but when noon came, I ate my own lunch, and after school, Alice walked home alone. We continued on for a few days after that, but we gradually eased apart. I don't think it ever occurred to her that she had done anything wrong.

Of course, there have been other girlfriends and many more disappointments since then, but 60 years later, that's the one I remember. Sometimes I wonder how her life turned out. If it matters, I also wonder how much she weighs now … but I hope she's happy. If she's not happy, I hope that at least she's full! ❖

First Schools, First Loves

By Jerrel Swingle

The picture measures about 4 by 6 inches and endured some rough handling before it wound up in the album. It has three creases across it, as if someone tried to make it fit in an envelope to mail to a distant relative.

The subject of the photo is my second-grade class at Citron Elementary School in Anaheim, Calif. Considering its age, the picture is remarkably clear and sharp. The photographer must have been very good, because no one is horsing around and everyone is smiling or grinning broadly.

The girls are seated on a bench, hands loosely clasped in their laps, ankles crossed demurely. The one on the far right, wearing the checkered skirt and loose jacket, the one with the elfin features and the light brown hair trimmed in a modest pageboy, is Doris Essery. Sweet and unassuming, she was my very first love. I couldn't tell you why exactly, but let's face it, love is hard to explain.

At some point during the school year, I decided I just had to be engaged to Doris. I had found a little ring as a prize in some penny candy, and it seemed to me to be a very good omen.

Mustering up what little courage I had, I waited to make my move until she was completely vulnerable. I'll never forget the moment. It was during afternoon recess, and the love of my life was hanging by her knees from an exercise bar on the playground. I nervously approached her, tossed the ring at her while she was still hanging there upside down, and then ran away as fast as I could, never looking back. She never really said whether she accepted my proposal, but she did wear the ring after recess.

The boys in the picture are standing in a row behind the girls. There are three little towheads, one cute Mexican boy whose incisors dominate his smile, and me and my very best friend, Johnny Ledbetter. I'm the one on the far left, looking like I'm trying to suppress a giggle. Doris is seated on the far right—probably sheer coincidence.

Citron School was not only the place where I had wonderful friends and fell in love with Doris; it was also the place where I fell in love with books and learning. I loved the rich smell of oiled wooden floors, chalk dust and new crayons. I liked the taste of graham crackers and cool milk at rest time, and of library paste when no one was looking. I loved all my teachers and the way they taught and cared for us. Their faces have blurred over the years, but the memory of their kindness and patience remains. When I had to leave the state in the middle of third grade, I felt a sense of loss that, even after all these years, has never entirely faded from memory.

My second-grade class at Citron Elementary School in Anaheim, Calif., circa 1935. I am on the far left in the back.

Now, as I look at that photograph and at the smiling faces looking back at me, I have to wonder what life might have been like had I stayed in California, in Anaheim, at Citron School, and even, maybe, with Doris. ❖

The Inkwell

By Donald J. Mikolajczak

The sign read, "Open House—St. Adalbert Elementary School." Although the building had been recently refurbished, I had hopes that some of the old flavor still remained. I was not to be disappointed. Looking at my sixth-grade classroom, I found the desks to be pretty much the same.

The iron was painted black and the oak desktops and seats had been refinished to a varnished luster. They looked better than my embellished memory could recall—except for the gaping hole in the upper right-hand corner where the inkwell would be. In the day of ballpoint pens, the inkwell was a vestige reflecting past endeavors.

Sister Ambrose announced that we were going to put aside our pencils and, except for arithmetic, everything we wrote would be in ink. We were given directions regarding what kind of nib or pen tip and pen holder to buy, and we were directed to purchase a few extra nibs for starters. Chances were we'd break a few before we learned how much pressure to apply when writing with ink.

A pig-tailed girl writes in her notebook. This photograph was taken at Tower Hill School in Wilmington, Del., in 1943. Photograph courtesy the Library of Congress, Farm Security Administration–Office of War Information Photograph Collection, LC-USW3- 053568-D.

The inkwell slide-by cover was to remain closed when not in use or the ink would evaporate. We began each day by practicing our Palmer Method of penmanship, making ovals and vertical strokes we called "sticks."

Sister warned us, saying, "The nibs will be scratchy, and most of you will make the mistake of using too much ink. This will result in drops, dribbles and small pools of ink." She added: "Continue to practice your ovals and sticks, and you'll find that your assignments will look less and less like a Dalmatian family picture."

Although we tried valiantly to use the scratchy pens, most of us ended up with blue-black hands for our efforts.

As luck would have it, I sat behind the most beautiful girl in class, Patricia. All the boys loved her beautiful brunet hair and the fact that she smelled of Lifebuoy soap. All girls were icky, except Patsy. She wore her hair in pigtails—long, shining pigtails. Those braids mesmerized me as they swished back and forth across my desk. I couldn't concentrate on the subject at hand, and often stayed after school to catch up.

My fascination with Patsy's hair knew no limits. It reached the point where I could almost predict when she would sit back and when those braids might sweep across my desk. I knew when they would swish left and when they would swish right. I thought that I probably had the most dust-free desk because Patsy overworked those pigtails.

"Did you ever want to dip Patsy's pigtails in your inkwell?"

I dreamed of touching those magnificent braids with my sweaty little palms, but I also knew that Patsy would never smile at me again if I did. And I'd die if I was deprived of her smile, even if only for a while.

One day, Frankie, who was always in trouble for something, asked me, "Did you ever want to dip Patsy's pigtails in your inkwell?"

Thinking that this was a case of boys vs. girls talk, I replied, "Yeah, all the time."

Then Frankie said, "If you do it, every boy in this class will give you a nickel. I'll see to it." Because the classroom bully and enforcer had established a reputation over the past six years, I figured that his offer was money in the bank. In fact, it sounded like I'd better attempt it, or else.

In the days that followed, Frankie asked me, "When are you going to do it?" He was getting impatient. I couldn't put him off any longer.

It wasn't long before Frankie's offer became a threat. "Look, stupid, because I'm such a nice guy, I'll give you a week to do it. Then I'm coming after you. It's dip or a knuckle sandwich." I knew what that meant. It meant that it was either Patsy's darling pigtail or a shot in the mouth from Frankie.

My week was almost up, and Frankie was looking more and more menacing. It was during religion class, when we all sat up straight and paid attention lest we burn in purgatory, that Patsy's pigtail rested on my desk next to the inkwell. It just sat there, *begging* to be dipped.

In a nonchalant manner, I opened the slide-by cover of the inkwell and gently dipped her braid in the ink. She felt something pulling her braid and began to turn. As she did, the slide-by cap of the inkwell snapped shut, catching her braid in the container. She gave a yank. The wet braid swung from the inkwell, hitting me right across the cheek, leaving an ink blot.

Sister Ambrose turned from the chalkboard to find the class silent and attentive. She knew that something had happened, but she didn't know quite what. The class was deathly quiet. Then a giggle broke out here and there. While Patsy daubed her pigtail with a tissue and I sat with an ink blot on my cheek, Sister had a good idea of what had happened. She knew that justice had been served.

One by one, during recess, each of the boys gave me a nickel. Frankie was there to see that everyone coughed up. He smiled and hit me on the arm when he paid his dues.

But as we were returning from recess, Sister Ambrose had the missions canister out on her desk. Then she asked me knowingly, "What are you going to do with all your newfound wealth?"

Surprised, I looked at Frankie, Sister, my nickels and Patsy. I gulped and answered, "Well, Sister, the sixth-grade boys were thinking of donating it to the missions." The whole class applauded, except for Patsy. As she turned to look back at me, she glowered at me. "Just wait," she said softly, so that only I could hear. "My turn is coming."

Seats were changed the following day. Patsy sat behind me. This earned me a jab with a pencil or pen for the rest of the semester whenever I gave an incorrect or stupid answer.

As I recovered from my reverie, I heard a vaguely familiar voice say, "Hello, I'm the sixth-grade teacher here at St. Adalbert. May I help you?" I turned to see a face from the past. Her smile still evoked a warm feeling inside me. It was Patsy, now Sister Patricia. Her hair, no longer braided brunet, now crowned her head like a silver halo under the bonnet she wore as part of her habit.

She smiled, saying, "It's true. They always return to the scene of the crime." ❖

The Visitor

By Kate Hartnell Stobbe

Corresponding with pen pals was a popular pastime when I was of junior-high age. Our English, history and geography teachers encouraged this exchange of letters. In fact, reading an interesting letter to our class from a "pal" was very acceptable, since it taught us about life in another city, town or state.

In English class we were asked to comment on the content, form, wordage and penmanship, etc., to give our overall thoughts on another's writings—not in a critical way, but only as a learning tool.

Some classmates corresponded with foreign students. It was a good way to learn about places outside our own country.

I had a pen pal who lived in Madison, Wis. We wrote to each other once a month or so. I always wondered, *Will we ever meet in person?* Our letters usually included an invitation to visit, but I always ended up thinking, *It probably never will happen.*

Her northern state took on a special meaning to me as I pored over maps and read extensively about its history. This interest didn't hurt my grades in the least.

One day in late April 1935, I received a letter from Wisconsin. June Brooke wrote that she and her aunt would be traveling to St. Louis, Mo., as soon as school was out, close to the end of June.

Their school in the north was in session longer than ours because of many snow days. Their semi-rural area was often snowbound for a week or more during a winter siege. (June had written that her parents had named her June because they looked forward to that month after a long, cold winter.)

Since St. Louis wasn't too far from our country home, my pen pal wrote that her aunt had said, "We may have time for a short visit to your friend's home if we can get a bus from where we are

1937 *The Farmer's Wife* magazine, House of White Birches nostalgia archives

in the city." She added that they both enjoyed traveling by bus very much and didn't wish to put us to any trouble. This trip, we knew, could easily be made, since city buses ran to our area on a regular basis.

To say that this news made me happy would be an understatement. My whole family helped with the plans to welcome June and her aunt. Hoping that their visit would last for a few days, we planned trips to local places of interest and ways to make their stay as pleasant as possible. Mother planned her very best meals, and Dad decided to paint the house a little sooner than he had originally planned.

June (right) and I are shown here about two years after we graduated from high school.

Eleanor, my little sister, would embroider a small pillow for both of them. I busied myself making a small booklet of memorable paragraphs that my pen pal had written, and my answers to her questions. The booklet was bound in blue construction paper with a gold cord and was titled *June's Questions. My Answers.*

By late June, our projects were near completion as we anticipated meeting our guests. Finally, on July 9, a phone call let us know that they would leave the city on the 12th at 12:30, and that they would arrive within an hour. We met them at the bus station. After two years of correspondence, June and I greeted each other as old friends would. Soon, we all felt like we'd known each other forever.

We had planned several entertainments for them during their three-day stay. On their second evening with us, Mother invited some of our neighbors and friends for a backyard picnic. After enjoying the food, June's aunt told us about the numerous Indian mounds near their home in Madison, where artifacts—remains of baskets, arrowheads, tools and pottery—were found. These were housed in the local museum. She knew much of the Indian lore, their history and even some of their language.

We, in turn, described our visit to the city, and seeing Charles Lindbergh's mementos of his nonstop flight across the ocean that were on display at the Jefferson Memorial. Our neighbors described tours and trips that they had enjoyed. It was a wonderful exchange.

All too soon, our happy meeting had to end. On our last evening together, as we chatted away like old friends on the front porch, June's Aunt Karry told us the reason for their trip to our area. It was to visit her twin sister, Mary.

They had been estranged for 20 years because of some silly family difference of opinion and had finally made their peace with each other. It was wonderful news.

Morning arrived all too soon. A few tears were shed at the breakfast table and as we drove our guests to the bus station. But they couldn't dampen the happiness we felt at having finally met in person. Our exchange of letters seemed so much more meaningful since we had met and grown to love each other as sisters.

June could not attend my high school graduation because her school was still in session. I traveled alone by train for her graduation, and her family treated me as if I were family.

Our friendship continued through letters, phone calls and visits. June was the matron of honor at my wedding, and we continue to be pen pals. She still resides in Madison, while I have moved to the westernmost city in Missouri. But regardless of distance, we will always be friends. ❖

Norman
Rockwell

Luck of the Draw

By Norma Gage

It was a cold morning in the autumn of 1944, and Miss Abbott's second-grade classroom was its customary quiet as she strolled up and down each aisle, a pointer in her hand. The only sounds were those of pencils and erasers scratching against paper, and the rhythmic ticking of the clock as its long, skinny arms moved around its face from one Roman numeral to the next.

Half-pint bottles of milk were lined up like little soldiers on the cool window ledge, ready for our daily mandatory nutrition break.

It was a rule that the arithmetic problems needed to be completed and the milk consumed before recess, or we would have to stay at our desks instead of playing outdoors with the other kids.

"Who would like to be the first to have a vaccination today?"

I always regarded arithmetic as an enemy bent on robbing me of my playtime. Gazing at the tall horse chestnut tree outside the window reminded me of the lovely swing hanging from its sturdy branch. I gazed outside, imagining thrilling rides high in the air with the breeze blowing through my long hair.

I also detested the taste of the slightly less-than-cold milk that offered a thick layer of cream on top. No matter how much I shook the bottle, the cream failed to homogenize into the milk. It floated in thick streaks, producing a taste not unlike the smell of my Uncle James' barn. As far as I was concerned, the only salvation for this icky stuff was to add some hot tea and honey. Then it held the promise of perfection!

I trembled as Miss Abbott's footsteps approached my desk. I knew that she would read over my shoulder and see how few problems I had completed. Survivors of her class told horror tales about getting rapped across the knuckles with the end of the steel-tipped pointer for working too slowly. I hadn't actually seen her do anything like that, but I was worried just the same.

She was within two desks of seeing my paper when the door opened and Miss Partridge, the school nurse, summoned Miss Abbott to the front of the room. All eyes focused on their whispering conversation. The two of them looked like they belonged in different worlds. Miss Abbot, in her flowing skirt and bright sweater, offered a sharp contrast to the nurse, who wore her traditional white starched uniform and a hat that looked like a doily.

They turned to face the class, and Miss Abbott commanded our attention by tapping the pointer against the edge of a desk.

Miss Partridge smiled and tried to force her squawking voice to sound pleasant: "Today is immunization day, children, and although your classroom was not scheduled to receive your smallpox protection until next week, Dr. McGinnis has just enough vaccine for two more inoculations."

Country Home magazine, Nov. 1934, House of White Birches nostalgia archives.

A wave of goosebumps flowed across my neck, and I crouched lower in my seat so that I wouldn't be seen. Yes, we were all very aware of the designated days for the public health department to visit the school for our free immunizations. It was a torture that adults had thought up for school kids to supposedly protect us from things we could hardly pronounce, let alone understand. Until that moment, the way I had it figured, I didn't have to be concerned about this threat for at least another seven or eight days.

But Miss Partridge continued, "Who would like to be the first students in the class to have a vaccination today?"

She had to be kidding! She acted like she was giving away a snazzy, new, balloon-tired bike! We were talking about *needles* stuck into our arms! Was she daffy?

Miss Abbott produced a small basket from a cupboard in the cloakroom and ordered each of us to write our name on a piece of paper and drop it in for "a fun drawing." Reluctantly, I folded my paper into as tiny a ball as possible and dropped it into the basket.

When she had collected them all, she returned to the front of the room and grinned as she went through the motions of mixing them all up. Miss Partridge closed her eyes and reached in to pull out a name. She opened her eyes and, with a huge smile, announced the winner, "Beatrice!"

I couldn't look at the poor girl, as I was certain she must be in tears. Beatty, as we called her, rose to her feet and stood leaning on the edge of the desk, her head bowed so low that her short bobbed hair swung forward. Surely there were tears hiding behind the curtain of blond draped over her eyes.

Then the next name: "Norma!" I felt numbness overtake my body! I couldn't image how my name had been picked out of all those tiny clumps of paper.

After a split-second of silence, applause broke out led by Miss Abbott as the so-called winners were summoned forward. Somehow I managed to convince my trembling legs to stand and propel me toward the front of the room. We were ushered out the door as the class continued to cheer in their relief at not having been chosen.

It was a long walk following Miss Partridge's echoing orthopedic oxfords as we clomped up two flights of stairs to the nurse's office. We trudged silently, like little zombies, in a manner suggesting that we were about to face a firing squad.

The doctor sat waiting for us by a table loaded with trays of syringes and needles. The odor of tincture and antiseptic attacked our nostrils. He greeted us with a smile and eyed our frightened faces over spectacles resting on the end of his nose. "Well," he said, "you managed to find a couple of very brave little girls." The implication that we might have to be courageous caused Beatrice to retreat farther behind me so that I would look like the logical choice to step up and be first.

Miss Partridge helped me take off my sweater. Then she rolled up the sleeve on my left arm. The doctor took hold of my arm and I felt a small scratch. At the same time, the doctor asked, "Tell me if you see the light blink."

I answered that I didn't and he stuck a Band-Aid on my arm. I glanced down in surprise, thinking that perhaps he had changed his mind about shooting me. But he just smiled and said, "That's all there is to it!"

"You mean you aren't going to stab me with one of those needles?"

The doctor's steel-gray eyes peered at me for a moment and he answered, "Not today."

Miss Partridge helped me put my arm back inside the sleeve of my sweater and walked me over to sit on the cot. Then her attention focused on Beatty, who had decided to make like an ostrich and bury herself in shyness with her fists frozen against her face. Miss Partridge was having a difficult time removing her sweater with Beatty's hands glued to her forehead.

I knew I would be speaking out of turn, but I had to let her know that this vaccination thing really didn't hurt. "Beatty, don't worry," I said. "It was easy. I didn't bleed or nuthin'." Miss Partridge put a finger to her lips to make me hush.

Finally, Beatty relaxed her arm, and in a flash the doctor had done his job.

Beatty opened her eyes and stared at me. She said nothing, but I could tell that she was thinking about us being scared out of our minds for no reason. Surprisingly, it had been a painless ordeal.

Miss Partridge walked us back just as the last of the kids exited our classroom for recess. She spoke briefly to Miss Abbott and then departed. I ran back to my seat to try and get the rest of my arithmetic done so I could have some recess time.

All of a sudden I heard Beatty start to cry. She stood by the window and complained tearfully that someone had drunk her bottle of milk. Miss Abbott scurried over to the case with all the empty milk bottles and pulled out a full bottle of the dreaded liquid.

Beatty started to smile, but Miss Abbott looked upset. "I'm sorry, Beatrice," she said, "but there appears to only be one bottle left, so we'll have to split it between the two of you." I leaped up from my desk and ran to Miss Abbott. I said, "She almost fainted and really needs it, so please let her have the whole bottle."

Miss Abbott nodded her approval and handed the warm bottle of milk to Beatty, who immediately pulled off the cardboard stopper, inserted the straw and began sucking up the stuff like it was some kind of sweet ginger ale. I stifled a gag as I watched.

As I started to return to my desk, Miss Abbott stopped me. "You know, Norma, I heard how brave you were getting your vaccination," she said, "and it was sweet of you to give up your milk for your friend. I am very proud of you. Why don't you run along outside and enjoy some fun on the swings for the remainder of recess? I'll excuse you from the balance of your arithmetic problems for today."

Even at that tender age, I knew I had just pulled a fast one. This teacher I considered very scary was now singing my praises as though I had just turned in a perfect arithmetic paper. My conscience knew that I was enjoying this flattery under false pretenses, but surely there would be plenty of time to straighten the whole thing out—right after a turn on the swing that would surely fly high into the large, droopy leaves of the horse chestnut tree.

This day had turned out to be pretty lucky after all. ❖

One Tough Boy

By Louis M. Tucciarone

In 1938 we moved from Brooklyn to Bethpage, Long Island, where farming was still one of the many sources of industry. It was spring, and the scent of manure mingled with the earth as the farmers plowed their fields, raising dust and disturbing the birds as they picked at the dried, wind-blown cornstalks that had withstood winter's icy chill only to be plowed under by man and his machine.

I was 12, in sixth grade, a city boy about to be introduced to country life. And it wasn't easy.

My first day in class is still a memory. I dressed for school as I had in Brooklyn: high-topped black shoes, neatly polished, blue serge knickers, red tie, white shirt and, of course, the jacket to match. Mom wanted to make sure I made a good impression.

The school was a two-story, red brick structure with eight classrooms, landscaped with swings and a baseball field. *Very nice,* I thought to myself as I entered the principal's office.

He wants them to believe that he is tough, but he is a very hurt boy.

He smiled very politely as he escorted me upstairs and introduced me to my homeroom teacher, Mrs. Hart. She, too, smiled very politely. "Class," she said, "this is Louis Tucciarone. He will be joining us this year." Everyone stared for a moment, then broke out laughing. I wanted to run and hide, but Mrs. Hart hit the desk with a heavy ruler and the class became quiet.

At lunch, I met some of the kids, and as I did, I realized why they had laughed at me. They all wore dungarees. Even some of the girls wore them. Frankie was the only boy who would talk to me. He was much shorter than the others, but what he lacked in height, he made up in spirit.

I managed to get through the day, but after school, the boys asked me if I would like to play baseball with them. I decided to do so. That was my first mistake. Then they asked me to be the catcher. Needless to say, they had an ulterior motive. By the time the game was over, my neatly pressed blue serge knickers were down to my ankles, with holes in the knees; in no way did I look like I had that morning. I still don't know where my tie is.

I became angry and started fighting with one of the boys. The rest all joined in, and by the time it was over, I looked like I had gone 15 rounds with Joe Louis. I heard one of them shout, "OK, he's had enough, let him go!" I sat there for a moment, my nose bleeding badly and one eye just about closed.

RAY C.
STRANG

Then I stood, and as I wiped the blood from my face, one of them came toward me. I took a wild swing and landed a punch on his left cheek. I stood over him and shouted, "What's the matter? Can't you fight one at a time?"

He stood up and shook his head. He glared at me with half a smile and said, "My name is Frankie. Wanna play ball again tomorrow?" I braced myself for another punch. Instead, he put out his hand and started to laugh. Everyone joined in laughing and put their hands out to me. For some strange reason, I did too.

During the next few weeks, Frankie and I became good friends. At the time, I didn't know why he had been held back for a year and had to struggle just to get C's. I always felt that if he hadn't been that cocky kid who "didn't take nothing from nobody," he probably wouldn't have made it in the sixth grade.

His dad had a farm, and many days during planting season, Frankie didn't show up for school. When that happened, he would ask me if I would like to go to his house after school and hang out for a while. I soon realized that he really wanted help with his homework. I didn't mind, because Frankie was special.

He had a terrible problem remembering dates from history.

One day when Mrs. Hart asked him, "When was the war of 1812 fought?" he just stared at her. He didn't even blink an eye; he just stared.

We made it through the sixth and seventh grades, but in the eighth grade he really had a problem. I became angry with him one day when we were working during recess. "What's the matter with you anyway?" I yelled. "Why can't you learn anything?"

He stood up and looked at me for a long time. His fists were clenched so tightly that his knuckles turned white. Remembering my first day at school, I braced myself, shouting, "Go ahead, take a punch at me if it makes you feel better!" But he just stood there. I could not understand it. Why hadn't he taken a poke at me?

I heard Mrs. Hart call my name. "Louis, you come here this moment!

"Do you know what you just did?" she said. "Do you have any idea at all what you did?" She always repeated herself when she was angry. "Do you have any idea how you hurt him?"

I stood there, surprised, unable to move. Then I asked, "What's the matter with him? What did I do wrong?"

"Don't you know?" she said, shaking me with both hands. "Don't you know?" I shook my head.

"Frankie has a learning disability. When he was a child he always loved to read. When he was in the third grade, he was caught reading when he should have been doing chores and his father beat him unmercifully. Since then, he hasn't been able to read and understand as well as you or any other student. But he tries so hard, Louis. He tries so hard."

I saw tears in her eyes. "Louis, you have been a terrific help to him," she continued. "He really needs you. You are the only real friend he has. Have you noticed how the other children don't bother with him? He wants them to believe that he is tough, but underneath, he is a very hurt boy. Louis, go to him. He needs you." She gave me a hug, then turned me around, whispering, "Go to him, Louis. Go to him."

I found him in our "thinking spot" under the porch behind the school, sitting with his knees against his chest, his arms wrapped around them. His chin rested on his knees as his eyes stared into oblivion. "Hey!" I shouted. "Mind if I join you?"

Startled, he looked at me. "Why not?" he replied. "It's a free country." We sat there for a while, in total silence, speaking unspoken words of understanding.

The next day we were pals again, and we made it through the eighth grade. I'll never forget the look on his face when he was told that he would graduate, and was recognized as the person who had worked hardest during the year.

Before we left for the summer, Mrs. Hart called me into her room. "Louis," she said, "you have done something very beautiful for Frankie. Remember: Yesterday is a memory, and tomorrow is a dream, but today, today is real."

Frankie graduated and joined the Marines in 1944. I moved to another town and lost track of him. But whenever I had a problem or struggled to learn something, I always thought of Frankie and "remembered when." ❖

. . . And Remember Me

By Hazel Hopkins Butts

Don't make love at the garden gate,
Love is blind but the neighbors ain't.

That sage advice is a sample of the wisdom recorded in three old autograph albums I came across this spring while cleaning out the closet in our back bedroom. Two albums were from my sixth- and ninth-grade graduations in 1943 and 1946, and the third, dated 1907, was from my mother's grade-school graduation.

All cleaning halted while I poured myself a cup of hot coffee, sank into a comfortable chair and leafed through them. Page after page held written bits of sentiment, humor and advice from friends, schoolmates, teachers and relatives.

Their universal theme was the desire to be remembered by the album's owner. A couplet penned in my sixth-grade album by a sister "grad-u-8" expressed that desire:

When you are old and sipping tea,
Take out this book and remember me.

Another not-so-thoughtful friend suggested:

When you are old and sipping tea,
Burn your tongue and think of me.

Other friends penned these comments:

In the forest there is a tree,
And on it it says, "Remember me."

If writing in albums remembrance assures,
With the greatest of pleasure I'll write in yours.

Above their signatures, teachers rarely wrote more than a word or two of greeting. They could hardly be blamed for rejecting long verses or quotations when their graduating classes numbered 200–300 students! Occasionally, a teacher with a literary bent would add a more extended word of advice or encouragement, as one of my sixth-grade teachers did:

May you live as long as you want,
And not want as long as you live.

At least two references were made to the Borough of Brooklyn, the location of my alma mater:

We've laughed a lot and talked a lot
and broken many a rule,
But oh, how could we help it,
in a Brooklyn public school?

Remember me and don't forget,
It was in Brooklyn we first met.

Penmanship in all three albums was usually exemplary. Some even bordered on calligraphy, including this modest entry:

My pen is poor, my ink is pale,
My hand shakes like a puppy dog's tail.

The script in the latter may have been exceptional, but the spelling and the punctuation told a different story. In the original couplet, that last line reads:

My hand shaks like a pupy's dog tail.

Girls tended to express their thoughts in sentimental verse, as did Laura and Dorothy:

No golden crown, oh Hazel, dear,
No costly gems have I.
But I've a wreath of love for thee,
That love can never die.

When the golden sun is setting,
And your mind from care is free,
When of others you are thinking,
Won't you sometimes
think of me?

Boys avoided sentimentality totally. They went to the opposite extreme when signing their sister graduates' albums. These lines contain excellent advice, but decidedly lack any romance:

When you are married
and live upstairs,
Don't get drunk
and fall downstairs.

In his autograph, my friend Joe, who had a taste for soft drinks, wrote:

1937 *The Farmer's Wife* magazine, House of White Birches nostalgia archives

If in heaven we don't meet,
You can blame it on St. Pete;
If perchance it gets too hot,
Pepsi-Cola hits the spot.

Both those verses were signed "Sincerely," and neither included any wish to be remembered. Both are nevertheless remembered with great affection.

Always be happy
and sing like a lark,
But never walk home
with a boy after dark.

When you get married
and your husband gets cross,
Pick up a broom
and show him who's boss.
When you get married
and have two twins,
Don't come to me for safety pins.

When you're in the kitchen
learning how to cook,
Remember it was Nancy
who wrote this in your book.

At least one or two of the traditional "Roses are red, violets are blue, sugar is sweet and so are you" quotations are in each of the albums. But there were also variations on that theme. In some, the "roses are red, violets are blue" line was followed by another version, including:

… I'm a graduate, so are you.
and,
… I've nary a friend nicer than you.

One girlfriend—and mind you, she was a close friend—wrote:

Roses are red,
and grass is green,
My face is funny,
but yours is a scream.

Another friend completely revised the original:

Roses are purple,
violets are white,
Ain't that crazy?

That friend was a 12-year-old boy who thought his lines were hysterically funny.

I agree.

Family autographs were a necessity in autograph albums. My mother chose to quote the psalmist when giving me her loving advice. It is advice I have tried to follow, although I have not always been successful:

"Trust in the Lord with all thine heart
and lean not unto thine own understanding.
In all thy ways acknowledge Him,
and He shall direct thy paths."

Doris wanted to be creative. She stewed and fretted for 10 minutes before inscribing these unforgettable words:

I hope your life will always be
as clean as a bald man's bean!

I also vividly recall the six giggling 10-year-olds who had been standing by during that creative process and who had squealed with delight upon hearing the lines read. I am still capable of a healthy giggle now and then, especially when reading words like these:

It tickles my toes
and makes me laugh,
To think you want
my autograph.

I laughed a bit and sniffled a bit as I read the messages in those albums. Each inscription had been recorded with bright hopes for the future and sage advice for enjoying it.

Too, I remember with joy the many beloved classmates, teachers, friends and family who took the time to express their caring by writing in my autograph albums. ❖

Cheater!

By Arlene Shovald

Whenever I see one of those old-fashioned French's mustard jars with the small opening, I remember the time back in grade school when I made what I thought was a beautiful geography project, only to be accused of cheating.

In the late 1940s, teachers, especially the nuns in the Catholic school I attended, were not always kind, loving figures kids could look up to. On the contrary, their word, right or wrong, was law, and if a student felt "picked on," it was just too bad. There was no going home to parents to complain, because most likely your folks would back up the teacher. That's just the way it was.

Our fifth-grade geography class was studying the Great Lakes. Now, I wasn't what you would call an A student. In fact, I was barely a C student, mostly because I found the lessons boring and uninteresting. (Today, I'd be diagnosed with attention deficit disorder, but in those days it was called "not applying yourself.")

"You took this water out of the faucet," she said. "You're a liar!"

But this particular subject was very interesting to me because we lived 100 miles from Lake Superior and Lake Michigan, and my Aunt Grace lived in Marquette, Mich., which is literally on the shore of Lake Superior. Our family was planning a weekend trip to visit Aunt Grace, and I knew that I could get lots of items from in and around the lake to create a special project and get extra credit.

Driving to Marquette was a big deal in those days. After all, it was 100 miles away, and that called for packing sandwiches and Kool-Aid in the picnic basket and stopping along the way for lunch. Even the dreaded carsickness I always experienced did not dim my enthusiasm.

When we arrived in Marquette, my cousin Laurel and I proceeded to Lake Superior where I collected the materials for my special project. Then Laurel's mom rinsed out a French's mustard jar for me, and I filled it with water from the lake. I was so proud! No doubt this would earn me an A—and besides, it was fun!

The next day was Sunday. After the long drive home from Marquette, I was still excited. I couldn't wait to start working on my Great Lakes project.

The square top from the cardboard box in which my winter boots had arrived served as the base. I filled it with sand from Lake Superior. Then I arranged stones I'd taken from the lake in a pile on one side. These stones were fascinating because they were as smooth as silk from the water washing over them.

Branches from the shoreline decorated my miniature beach. And finally, in one corner, I set the bottle of water labeled "Lake Superior

Water." Then I sat down to write my report about the largest of the Great Lakes—which states and provinces line its shores, and all the other facts I'd accumulated in my study.

On Monday morning I was extra careful as I brought my project to school. When the red, white and blue school bus stopped to pick me up, I handed my project to the driver while I climbed up the steps and took my seat in front. I held the box on my lap with both hands so as not to spill it.

I made it to school with no mishaps. I proudly placed my project on the windowsill, confident that it was the best. After all, who else was going to actually go to Lake Superior and bring back lake water in a jar? I couldn't wait for geography class to start!

Sister Rosita walked up and down the outside aisle, carefully looking over the projects. When she picked mine up, I was elated! She brought it to my desk and sat it in front of me.

I must have been smiling from ear to ear. And then the bubble burst.

"You took this water out of the faucet," she said. "You're a liar!" I couldn't believe what I was hearing! It had never *occurred* to me to take water out of the faucet and claim it was from Lake Superior!

My brother, Larry, and me on a trip to Marquette, Mich., circa 1949. I collected water from Lake Superior for a science project and was accused of taking it from the faucet.

I don't remember if I tried to defend myself. Probably not. That just wasn't done in those days. Children simply did not "talk back," especially to the nuns. Nor do I recall telling my parents, because "carrying tales" also was not allowed.

Time passed and there were other classes that called for special projects. I never made another one. But my experience became helpful when Harold, a talented boy in my class, suffered a similar situation.

We were studying the North or South Pole, and Harold brought in a beautiful extra project with penguins and polar bears he had carved from soap. A mirror in the center represented water, and stacks of Ivory Snow soap flakes were piled around the mirror to represent snow.

Sister Rosita picked up Harold's project and held it up in front of the class. "You didn't carve these figures!" she declared accusingly. "Your father did it. How dare you cheat!" Then she slammed the project onto Harold's desk.

I thought Harold was going to cry, but he managed to hold back his tears. Harold's father was an artist, so it was understandable that Harold would do good work. He obviously took after his dad. Why didn't the sister realize that?

During recess, I caught up with Harold. I told him it was a good thing that Sister had thought his father did the work. "That shows your work was very good," I said.

"You really think so?"

"I know so," I said. "It's so good she thinks your dad did it!"

Harold was a kid who would have benefited from a moment in the spotlight, but Sister Rosita missed that opportunity. It could have been a very special time for him.

While these experiences with the Lake Superior water and Harold's beautiful, hand-carved soap figures were not pleasant, they did teach me a valuable lesson. As a result, I never assume that anyone, particularly a child, is being dishonest without giving it a little more thought and investigation.

It never occurred to me—or to Harold—to be dishonest. We were kids! We were taught to always tell the truth. And it was a big shock to discover that the very adults who preached truthfulness must have practiced deceit themselves; otherwise, why would they have doubted us? It was a lesson in growing up that I never forgot. ❖

The Pencil Box

By Frances Beames

That Christmas, my present was a pencil box. What I really wanted was a Shirley Temple doll, but I knew better than to ask for it. Shirley Temple dolls didn't come cheap ($10 in the mail-order catalog, "in presentation box, shipping included"), and I might just as well have gone out and howled at the moon as mention such a thing. We were a large family on a small farm in the "Dirty '30s," so I got a pencil box and knew I should be thankful.

The pencil box was actually quite nice, once I got over its not being a doll. It was a double-decker of polished hardwood, about 2 x 2 x 8 inches. You could slide the lid back to reveal five grooves, each containing a yellow 2B pencil, or you could slide out the bottom part that was deeper; it held my crayons and an eraser. The crayon set was special, with a turquoise and a pale green that ordinary boxes of crayons did not possess.

At the back of the pencil box was a round hole, perhaps meant for an ink bottle. But as I was too young to write with pen and ink, the little well housed other things: a (used) stamp of the young princesses, Elizabeth and Margaret; a brass thumbtack; and the notes that were passed back and forth between my friend Mike and me.

The box was actually quite nice, once I got over it not being a doll.

Mike's real name was "Arlene." She was a big girl, slow to anger but mighty in her wrath, and although I was a year older, I felt lucky to have her as friend and protector. Anytime another kid made fun of my made-over dresses and hand-knitted stockings (including a pair made from leftover maroon wool, which caused me untold grief), Mike would tower over my tormentor and growl, "So?" and the teasing would stop. Even the Griersons were afraid of her.

Hartley Grierson was caretaker of the one-room school. He and his kid brother, Allan, were supposed to come early, unlock the door, fill up the drinking-water container, and in winter, light the fire to warm the place up. But it never really warmed up. The Griersons didn't get to school much earlier than the rest of us, and we could still see our breath when we came inside.

We used to put our desks around the stove in a circle, and the boys would put the soles of their rubber boots against the stove. This made a disgusting smell, and it earned them an occasional crack on the head from one of the older girls, which never stopped them from doing it. The teacher, Miss Donaldson, wisely ignored all of this.

At the time, I thought that she ignored far too much of what the boys were up to. In later years, however, I realized that for a young city girl dropped into this farm community, she managed us brilliantly.

And I trusted her enough to tell her as soon as I realized my pencil box was missing.

It was a Monday morning. I put my hand into my desk as usual—nothing. I scrunched down and peered into the desk, but the pencil box simply wasn't there. I sat for a few minutes, silent and stunned. Stealing simply did not happen around our village, where people did not lock their doors or their cars.

The school was supposed to be locked, but it was only a token locking. Anyone could have opened any window without the aid of burglar tools. But someone who came in the window would have stolen something more, like the school bell, or—well, there wasn't anything much to steal, come to think of it. And a stranger wouldn't have known about my nice pencil box.

There were only 15 kids in the school, and I figured the thief had to be one of the younger ones. Older students would not steal, because what could you do with a stolen pencil box? You couldn't use it in school. You couldn't take it home; your parents would notice and you'd be in trouble. You couldn't show it off to your friends; they'd tell. So what would be the point? Only a young, stupid kid would have taken it. But who would have had the chance? Who was in school when the rest of us were not?

I remembered Allan's covetous eyes on my splendid pencil box, and instantly knew as sure as God made little green apples that he had been unable to resist temptation. But how to get it back? At recess, I went to Miss Donaldson and told her about my great loss.

"You're quite, quite sure he's the one?"

I nodded. "I thought maybe you could go and look in his house."

She shook her head. "Well, no, I couldn't do that. It wouldn't be right. We'll have to think of some way to make him want to bring it back."

"He'll never want to bring it back, because then everyone will know he took it. He'll probably throw it in the creek."

I could feel my eyes filling at the very idea—my lovely pencil box going into the muddy, cold creek.

"What if you put up a poster offering a reward to whoever finds your pencil box?"

"*Pay* him to give it back?" I was outraged. Still, it seemed the only way.

That afternoon, Miss Donaldson announced the loss of my pencil box, noting that it might have fallen out of my school bag on the way home. She asked the seniors to make posters during their art class, one for the school and one for the general store at our crossroads, and they fell to. After awhile I even started enjoying myself, sitting with the senior class, describing what the pencil box looked like and what was in it.

Miss Donaldson said she would contribute 25 cents for the reward. I felt sure my dad would come up with the same, and I was rather pleased to think that my pencil box merited a bounty of 50 cents.

When we left school that afternoon, the Grierson boys ran on ahead, hoping to find the pencil box somewhere along the road, they said. Next morning, to the surprise of the other students, Allan appeared with my box and triumphantly claimed his reward from Miss Donaldson. I retrieved my lost treasure rather ungraciously, but managed to mutter a thank-you. The pencil box, on examination, seemed to have come to no harm.

The incident might have ended there, but during art class that afternoon, I happened to glance over at Allan's desk and saw him industriously crayoning a landscape with a turquoise sky! I don't remember leaving my seat. I only remember standing at his desk, speechless with rage, stabbing my indignant finger at his picture. Allan put his face down on his drawing. A dark red wash of color flooded his neck and came up over his ears. Then, slowly, a grimy hand offered up the turquoise crayon.

I didn't even look around for Mike's help. I took the crayon with my left hand and with my right fist thumped his head down on the desk as hard as I could.

Miss Donaldson, involved with the eighth grade and long division, must have seen this exchange, but although her lips twitched, she turned away without comment.

I sat down again and checked out the turquoise crayon. It wasn't broken. I didn't bother to check out Allan's nose. ❖

Marble Memories

By Joseph Kistner

In the 1920s, almost every boy in our school played marbles. Our school was the old College Avenue School in Poughkeepsie, N.Y. We played marbles whenever we could, during recess and noon hour at school and after school.

I had a large box of marbles when I was 8 years old. Much of my success was due to the marble I used for shooting. It was milky white with no blemishes, and it was heavier than the other marbles. A shooter like mine was called a "real" by marble players. It was one of my most prized and envied possessions.

We played two versions of marbles. In one, we drew a square on the ground and put marbles on each corner and one in the middle of the square. Then we tossed our shooters toward the square from about 12 feet away. The owner of the shooter closest to the square shot first and won the marbles he shot out of the square. If the marble was missed or, when hit, went into the square, it counted as a miss and the next player shot. This went on until the square was empty. Then the game continued, with another set of marbles in the corners and in the middle.

The other game of marbles was called "Baby in the Hole." We dug a round hole about 4 inches in diameter and surrounded it with marbles belonging to each player. The player closest to the hole after we tossed our shooters shot first and others followed in turn. The idea was to shoot marbles into the hole until one didn't go in. Then the next player shot.

Just about every boy carried a pocket full of marbles to school each day, starting about the middle of April. We wore knickers and still wore our long underwear because our mothers decreed we had to until the first of May. By then, the underwear had been washed so many times and stretched so much that it hung loosely on our legs. I remember wrapping the loose underwear around my legs when I put my socks on. The result was laughable. We all had lumpy legs under those socks to go with the lumpy pocket where we kept our marbles.

Some boys didn't take part in our marble games on the school grounds, but only watched from nearby. Then, when the bell rang to end the recess or noon hour, they would run to the nearest game and attempt to scoop up the marbles on the ground while yelling, "Ground Granchins!" Then they would try to escape us by running into the school.

I have no idea what "Ground Granchins" meant, but it was a yell that we guarded against. We were prepared to snatch up our marbles first. If we didn't, we chased the boys who did, and fisticuffs ensued unless they gave them back.

Hughey was one of the boys who lived in my neighborhood. He was about two years younger than I was and he liked to play marbles. He had about 100 marbles, so I decided to win a few of them.

The first time we played, I won all of his marbles in about an hour. When I won the last of them, Hughey began to cry. I felt sorry that I had taken them, so I gave them back and he stopped crying. The next time we played, the same thing happened, so from then on, we played for fun. Hughey grew up to be the chief of police in Poughkeepsie. Often, when I saw him, I would think about our marble games.

As my friends and I grew older, we found other games like baseball and football to occupy our time, and marbles were left to the younger boys. I gave my marbles, including my "real," to the boys in the neighborhood. I wish I had kept that marble as a reminder of the days when life was simple. It probably won some boy a box of marbles, as it did for me—at least I like to think it did, as I recall my marble memories. ❖

Albert & the Bully

By Audrey Corn

Practically every kid in the fifth grade liked Albert. Albert was small for his age, and skinny. And he wasn't a fighter. But he never had any reason to fight—until Butch Williams came along.

We had several bullies in our class back in the 1940s when I attended school in Brooklyn, N.Y. Butch was the meanest of the lot. And Albert was his favorite victim.

Butch poked fun at Albert's hand-me-down clothes and his thick eyeglasses. He called Albert a shrimp and a sissy, and whenever he got the chance, he tripped him. Albert endured Butch's bullying for a long time. My schoolmates and I figured Albert had little choice. My schoolmates and I were wrong.

"Not here, you dimwit," Butch said. "Later, after school."

One fine day, Albert blew his stack. Our class had gone out to the schoolyard for recess. Teacher stood on the sidelines, watching us play. Butch knew Teacher couldn't focus her attention everywhere at once, and he seized the opportunity to sneak up behind Albert and punch him.

Butch's victims usually turned tail and ran like scared rabbits. But this time, Albert angrily held his ground.

"You pimple-faced creep!" Albert shouted.

"Take that back, you little squirt!" Butch roared back at Albert.

"And what if I don't?" Albert sneered.

"I'll bash your head in, that's what!"

Word spread quickly, and a crowd quickly gathered. Albert ignored the gathering crowd. "You wanna fight?" he said. "OK, we'll fight." Albert balled up his fists.

"Not here, you dimwit," Butch said. "Later, after school."

"Now!" Albert bellowed.

"Don't be a jerk. Teacher's standing right over there! She'll see us," Butch hissed.

"You phoney baloney. You're scared!" Albert taunted. He raised his fists and charged the tormentor at full speed.

Butch hopped aside. He wasn't stupid enough to fight in front of the teacher. But he didn't intend to become Albert's punching bag, either. Butch's sideways leap should have placed him well out of harm's way. But Albert was no ordinary opponent. Albert had never engaged in fisticuffs in his life. He swung wildly. And he caught Butch square in the nose!

The rest of us stood speechless. Who'd have thought that puny little Albert could act so bravely? Not only did Albert stand up to Butch and bloody his nose, but he also had the guts to punch out Butch in front of Teacher. Teacher ordered Albert to return to the classroom to wait for her. She sent Butch to the nurse. As for the rest of us, she said that she expected us to behave like ladies and gentlemen.

Butch came back from the nurse's office wearing a big Band-Aid across his nose. Nobody knew exactly what happened between Teacher and Albert. Some said that Teacher sent a note home to Albert's parents. Others insisted that Albert instead had to write 500 times, "I will not victimize a fellow pupil."

Then a rumor began to circulate. According to this story, Teacher had encouraged Albert to stage his fight in the hopes of ending Butch's bullying. According to this rumor, Albert received no punishment whatsoever.

The bullying did stop. Butch told anyone who'd listen that Albert was crazy. Butch said no one in his right mind would willingly pick a fight in front of Teacher. Well, if Albert was crazy, he was crazy like a fox. I still wonder sometimes what really happened. But, like so many events from my past, Albert's secret lies buried forever back in the Good Old Days. ❖

The Shiner

By Neal Murphy

I never saw it coming. I turned around and my eye hit the knuckles of his right hand. I was 12 years of age, and this was my first fight at school. I guess it must not have been much of a fight. I don't remember seeing any blood or skinned places on this kid named Youngblood who had hit me.

In East Texas schools in 1948, not many student fights took place. Sometimes when you were "double dog dared" you might have to meet someone after school on the courthouse square and settle your differences. But we seldom fought on the school campus; I think the reason was the teachers, who were allowed to discipline us without fear of retribution from angry parents or adversarial lawyers.

My eye immediately began to swell and turn blue. As I have often stated, God works in mysterious ways, his wonders to perform, and that was the case with this incident. My parents were driving by the school campus on their way home for lunch when they spotted me sitting on the school fence. When they stopped, I told them what had happened. After assurances that my eye would be fine in a few days, they took me home and put some ice on it for the rest of the day.

I am pictured at age 12.

I was in the sixth grade at the time, and punishment for fighting was a sure thing. My homeroom teacher was Mrs. Dan Lowe. She called me into her office and handed me a piece of paper.

"Now, Neal," she said, "you know it is against school rules to fight for any reason. What you have to do is to memorize the poem on that paper. That's part one of your punishment. Part two is that you must go to every classroom in the school and say the poem in front of the class. I will be with you to make sure that you do."

Talk about cruel and unusual punishment! I thought that had been outlawed by the Constitution! But I had no choice; I had to do as I was instructed. I did memorize the poem, and I did recite it in each and every classroom in the school. I still have that poem, and I'd like to share it with you here:

A Gentleman

I knew him for a gentleman
By signs that never fail.
His coat was rough and worn.
His cheeks were thin and pale.
A lad who had his way to make,
With little time for play.
I knew him for a gentleman
By certain signs today.

He met his mother on the street,
Off came his little cap.
My door was shut, but he waited
Until I heard his rap.
He took the bundle from my hand,
And when I dropped my pen,
He sprang to pick it up for me,
This gentleman of 10.

He does not push and crowd along,
His voice is gently pitched.
He does not fling his books around
As if he were bewitched.
He stands aside to let you pass,
He always shuts the door.
He runs errands willingly
To forge, and mill, and store.

He thinks of you before himself.
He serves you if he can,
For in whatever company,
The manners make the man.
At 10 or 40, 'tis the same.
The manners told the tale,
And I discern the gentleman
By signs that never fail.

I do not know the author of this little poem, but it served its purpose with me. Mr. Youngblood and I never fought again.

Our schools did not have campus police, grief counselors, metal detectors, free breakfasts and lunches, or problems with lawyers. They were composed of dedicated teachers, helpful parents and students who were generally respectful of each other. But when, occasionally, there was a fight on campus, it was dealt with promptly. In my case, I still remember the fight and the punishment, even after some 58 years. Is there a message in there somewhere? ❖

Facing page: 1930 Listerine ad, House of White Birches nostalgia archives

JOHN FALTER

Beyond the Classroom

Chapter Five

My fondest recollections of school back in the Good Old Days weren't just bound up in the classrooms of the small rock schoolhouse I attended in southwest Missouri. Many of those "dear old golden rule days" were accented by all of the games, clubs and dances that went on beyond the classroom.

Today all of the activities after the ringing of the last bell of the day would be called "extracurricular."

We just called it fun.

Today all of those activities would be called "extracurricular."

It's pretty easy to understand why all of that activity beyond the classroom was so important to us country kids. For a lot of us, our lives were divided into three neat little compartments: family, church and school.

While family and church had a huge impact on our lives, it was at school that we spent the lion's share of our days. I have thought many times that the principles we learned from parents and preachers were put to the real world test at school and beyond the classroom.

School activities taught us to share, whether it was the only teeter-totter on the playground or the only baseball with a cover still on it. There we learned to be patient with those who were a little slower, a little more awkward or a little less talented. And we learned to be thankful when someone was patient with *us* for the same reasons.

I learned at home and at church that it was good to turn the other cheek. "A soft answer turns away wrath," said the minister, quoting from the book of Proverbs, "but grievous words stir up anger." But it was at recess on the basketball court when I was knocked flat that I discovered what that meant.

It would have been easy to spring to my feet and jump onto the back of the flagrant fouler. Of course, that would have succeeded in getting me thrown out of the game and banished to the school room by the omnipresent teacher and her whistle. So, a quick apology from the brute and an outstretched hand to help me to my feet was all it took to turn away my wrath.

By the end of the day we were fast friends.

And then there were the affairs of the heart. In the classroom many of us spied the loves of our lives, but it was beyond the classroom that we worked up the courage ask for or accept a date.

The first date I ever had was to my "Senior Banquet." We didn't have a prom in those days, since dancing was considered sinful. That was fine with me, since I had not a clue how to dance anyway. I spent the evening with enough perspiration pouring off me to convince my poor date that I probably had been jitterbugging on the sly.

But, on the other hand, that first foray into the romantic world helped prepare me for the time, just four years later, when I would meet the love of my life, my dear wife Janice.

These stories will take you on the trips, to the dances and with the teams to the time before and after the ringing of the school bells. Reading them, you will remember why an important part of our educational program was that which happened beyond the classroom.

—Ken Tate

SCHOOL
SLOW
Hughes

The Safety Patrol

By Michael Gelcius

Our public school is about three blocks from my house. Neighborhood schoolchildren are escorted across the busier intersections by crossing guards who are primarily senior citizens or mothers of the older children. This had me thinking about how things were different in my day. Back in my old hometown, we had the Safety Patrol.

My first school, where I attended kindergarten through fourth grade, was Franklin School in Kearny, N.J. It was a small, square, red brick building with an adjacent gravel schoolyard.

A busy county road ran along the east side of the property, and smaller town roads along the north and west. My house sat right across the street from the north end.

Because of the traffic volume in the area, and the fact that there were no traffic lights on any of the local roads at the time, the school had established a Safety Patrol to escort younger kids across busy intersections on their way to and from the building. The patrol wasn't made up of adults, though; it was made up of the fourth-graders. Each June, as the school year came to a close, third-grade boys and girls were asked if they wanted to be on the Safety Patrol for the following year. Those who were interested put their names on a list, got their parents' signatures on a permission slip, then hoped to be notified just before the new school year started.

It was the captain's job to make sure that everyone was at his or her post.

I don't know what criteria were used during the selection process, but my guess is that the third-grade teachers had the greatest say in who made the cut and who didn't.

I can't tell you how happy I was when I found out that I was going to be on the Safety Patrol. It was the spring of 1949, and one of the few times in my life that I couldn't wait for the new school year to begin.

There was only one concern. Mrs. Lamont, the fourth-grade teacher, was in charge of the Safety Patrol. She was a strict disciplinarian and had a reputation throughout the school as someone to be feared. She was the one who handed out the street corner assignments, and it was rumored that if Mrs. Lamont didn't like your looks, you'd be off the patrol before you could blink. As is the case with most childhood rumors, the "facts" were all wrong. But we didn't know that.

On the morning of the second day of school, the Safety Patrol met for the first time. Everyone was to report to the school hall a half-hour before classes started to receive instructions and be issued their patrol belts and street assignments.

For some reason, I arrived late. Mrs. Lamont was just finishing up and dismissed the group. My heart sank. I just knew that this was the end of my career. I sheepishly walked over to her and apologized for being late. I asked what my assignment was, then waited for her to tear off all my buttons and drum me out of the regiment.

I nearly fell over when she said, "I hope you're not going to be late all the time. I want you to be captain of the Safety Patrol."

Me? Captain? I didn't know what to say. I just stammered "Thank you!" and assured her that I would never be late again. And I never was.

It was the captain's job to make sure that everyone was at his or her post on time, to fill in at a post if one of the kids was out sick, and to keep a logbook of everyone's performance. After each morning's patrol and before class, I'd fill in the log, noting if each person was present, late or absent.

Each morning we gathered in the school hall to start our day. We put on our Safety Patrol belts, took roll call, said the Pledge of Allegiance, then marched out to our posts. We stationed two people at each corner along the county road, Schuyler Avenue. One person took the north corner and the other the south. We marched as a group, leaving two at each post as we proceeded along the way—first the corner of Bergen Avenue, then Wilson Avenue, Devon Terrace, Hoyt Street, Tappan Street and finally Dukes Street. The blocks were long, so when the bell sounded to come in, we had to signal from one post to the next to get everyone back.

The job of Safety Patrolman was rather simple. We reported for duty one hour before school each day and stayed at our posts for one hour after school. We waited for the schoolchildren to come along, then checked traffic and escorted them across the intersection. We never tried to control the flow of traffic. We just waited until it was safe to cross.

Sometimes other fourth-graders felt insulted by the suggestion that they needed an escort. But most kids just accepted the fact that we were doing our job and didn't give us a hard time. Even adults that came by would let us help them cross.

The school had rain gear and galoshes that we could borrow during bad weather. The heavy, yellow, rubberized hats and coats were the kind normally associated with fishermen in the North Sea. Most of us had enough sense to dress accordingly before going to school when the weather was bad, but we liked to wear the yellow slickers and hats because it was like wearing a uniform.

One of the perks of being on the Safety Patrol was receiving free movie tickets. Half of the squad got tickets one week and the other half the following week. I always made sure my close friends got their tickets the same week that I did so we could go to the movies together. The tickets were good for one admission to the Saturday matinee, and we never missed a show.

At the end of the school year, all of the fourth-grade patrols from the different schools gathered for an awards ceremony at the Garfield School auditorium. Each and every member of the Safety Patrol had his or her name read and was presented with a pin—gold for a perfect attendance record, silver for a good record and bronze for everyone else. They also gave each of us a raffle ticket; those whose numbers were called got to pick out a gift from the stage. There were plastic models of cars and planes, dolls, jewelry, bags of marbles, fancy tops, harmonicas and many other items. And you didn't need too much luck; everyone got to pick a gift eventually. The advantage came in having your number called early so that you had more to choose from. My number was called early, and I selected a model of an F-4U Corsair fighter plane.

Being on the Safety Patrol was a great experience. It taught me responsibility, and I took pride in working with my fellow patrolmen as a team and doing a job right. It was my first experience with community service, and I wouldn't have traded the time we spent for any amount of money. I think back very fondly on those hours and the good times we had. Those were the Good Old Days. ❖

Papa's Watch

By John L. Calamaro

When my father came to this country he had three things that never could be replaced. The first was my mother. He would hold her hand and tell anyone who would listen, "With this hand she can make a meal fit for a king, heal a person who is sick and clean a house so you can eat off the floor."

The second was me. He called me "Sonny Boy" and told me time and time again how the sky opened the day I was born. An angel came down carrying me in its arms and told Papa that someday I would be a great man.

In gratitude, the duke had the watch and medal made for Grandpa.

The third was his beloved watch. It was solid gold with a gold chain and a gold medal of St. Patrick, the patron saint of Ireland. The watch was given to him when his father died. Over and over, we had heard the story of how Grandpa had saved a man from drowning in County Cork. The man was an English duke who was visiting Ireland. Grandpa dove into the water and saved the duke. In gratitude, the duke had the watch and medal made for Grandpa. Now, it was Papa's pride and joy.

I began school in 1923 in Jersey City, N.J., and from the first day I loved to learn everything I could. When I was in the sixth grade, we were told to write a composition for a national contest. The theme was "What This Country Means to Me." I was one of three winners from New Jersey. We were to go to Washington, D.C., for the conclusion of the contest.

It was an honor to be a finalist in the competition, but I knew that we couldn't afford to travel to Washington, D.C., much less buy me new clothes. So I didn't tell my mother and father anything about it. My father worked in a factory making stoves. The work was very hard, and the pay was just enough to feed us and pay the rent. There never was any money left over for Mom to buy a dress or for Papa to get new work shoes; his old ones had holes in the soles.

Then one day, when school was over for the day and I was downstairs playing, my teacher, Mrs. Johnson, came over to our apartment to talk to my mother and father about going to the competition. My parents were sitting at the table when I came upstairs to eat. Papa looked at me and asked why I hadn't told them about the composition. I replied that it was nothing, "just something that I wrote and a few people think that it's good. That don't mean that I have a chance to win."

The next day was Saturday and Papa worked a half-day. When he came home, he took my mother and me to the ferry for New York City. When we got off, we made our way to Canal Street. My father had us wait outside while he went into a store. When he came out, we walked till we found a clothing store that had just suits, and my father picked a dark blue suit for me. Then we went to a shoe store and got a new pair of black wing-tip shoes. The next stop was a store that had all kinds of clothes. There we found a white shirt, a light blue tie and a dress for Mom.

We stopped at a small restaurant, and my father ordered meals for us and a bottle of wine. He then gave me a small glass of wine and said that we must observe this occasion. He looked at me with a smile and said, "Didn't I tell you that an angel gave you to us and said that you would be a great man, my Sonny Boy?"

I went to Washington. I didn't win, but I came in second, and it opened the way for me to go on and become a lawyer. My papa and mother lived to see me get my degree. They say it was their best day, watching me with love getting that degree. But to me, the day my papa sold his pride-and-joy watch to send me to my future was true love in its greatest form. ❖

28
Eugene Iverd

My Football Career

By R.C. Tuttle

During the early 1920s and 1930s, I lived in a small town on Long Island Sound, about 30 miles from New York City. Our home was across the street from a stretch of rolling grassland that served as the town's public park, and was the scene of sandlot baseball and football games. During winter we went there to skate on the frozen duck pond and enjoy sleigh riding. My own football career began in that park when I was in grammar school.

We kids played our own version of football on a flat, grassy section. Our game was tackle, without the uniforms and with little attention to the rules. (There were rules?) Our ages ranged from 8–12, and any number could play.

Each day after school we chose up sides. A backfield was picked, plays were developed on the spur of the moment, and we kicked off. Plays, which were actually quite creative, were usually a run through the line or around the end and the forward pass. We even tried the old Statue of Liberty play. However, the original running play was usually scrapped en route, and whoever had the ball plunged into a briar patch of grasping hands or tried a pass.

That's me out there at quarterback, poised for the game-winning toss!

Some of us became quite adept at tossing a pass from under a pile of bodies. "Blocking" quickly became pushing and holding, whereas "tackling" was wrestling the runner to the ground by any means possible. It was difficult to tell the difference between offense and defense. Also, some of the younger players often forgot which team they were on and attacked anyone who had the ball.

We had more success with the forward pass. As for kicking, most of the time the ball ended up either out in the road or in nearby bushes. Or, the kick was blocked.

When I was in the backfield, I favored the pass despite the "rough-the-passer" attitude we all had adopted after watching numerous high-school games. One of my best friends took keen delight in flattening me while I tried a pass.

Our goal lines were marked by a couple of rocks and tended to be moved during the game, so scores were subject to doubt. Also, not having goal posts, we ran through the line or passed for the extra point. It was quite a melee. We played until dark, then went home, a tired but happy bunch. Scores were meaningless, and we all accepted the rough stuff—in fact, we reveled in it. This fun, harmless, rough-and-tumble activity probably helped toughen us up for the years ahead.

Later, in the seventh and eighth grades, our school fielded a more organized football team, and I quickly joined up. We had uniforms, and a coach who insisted that we learn the basic moves of the game. I hadn't grown much during those early years and usually played in the backfield on the second team, occasionally substituting in the first-team games.

We had a regular schedule and played other schools and YMCA teams. When the turf froze in the fall, our practice field was similar to a cement parking lot. But between playing in the informal and formal versions of the game, we all picked up some skills in blocking, tackling and kicking. Actually, I still preferred the grassy public-park version where, oddly enough, nobody got hurt; it seemed players were always getting banged up in the school games.

Our school team won some and lost some and wound up the season with a football dinner and speeches by the stars. I was never asked to give a speech. I contented myself with the creamed chicken on toast and the comment "You fellows were the best team we ever had!"

My friends and I still occasionally enjoyed a pickup game at the park under our old rules. (What rules?) During those days, I was a fan of college football, as were my parents. Dad had a cousin who was a Yale graduate, and he often sent tickets to games in New Haven's Yale Bowl.

I recall watching Albie Booth and Chris Cagle in Yale-Army games. Most people along the East Coast remember Albie Booth of Yale, but I'll bet very few remember Chris Cagle, the Army quarterback. They were stars during the mid-1920s. Both were small in stature; their success was based on their ability to react, their accurate passing, and their skill in worming their way through a well-muscled line.

Both were almost impossible to tackle. I enjoyed watching those two little guys playing against each other. Albie Booth lived and worked in New Haven after graduation. I don't know what happened to Chris Cagle; I've often wondered.

My father graduated from Springfield College in 1913 and had been a good drop kicker—a skill long since departed from modern football. He lived to be 96, a football fan to the end.

During the 1920s, on Saturday afternoons, we listened to football games on the radio. Then, in the evenings, we'd listen to scores from around the country. Notre Dame was the football powerhouse during the 1920s—the Four Horsemen, Knute Rockne, the Gipper, etc. Most of the time they savaged their opponents. However, there was one memorable Saturday when the West Point Cadets creamed them.

For some reason, we were fans of Slippery Rock Teachers College—we were probably fascinated by the name—and for obvious reasons, we never missed the Springfield College results.

I still enjoyed the game when I was in high school, but I found the practice too time-consuming. I was interested in music; I played trombone in the band and piano in the high-school orchestra. So, after a week of football practice, I quietly turned in my uniform and thereafter limited my high-school sports to the shot and discus on the track team.

1933 *Farmer's Wife* magazine, House of White Birches nostalgia archives

Our high-school team had some good players who quickly became local heroes, giving life to the popular song *You've Got to Be a Football Hero to Get Along With the Beautiful Girls*. And they did. A mere trombone player, on the other hand, was generally ignored.

I also became a member of the YMCA that fielded a football team. I found the experience to be much like that of my earlier public-park football. We had moved to town, and I lived just a few minutes from the Y field. Usually about

14–15 fellows came to practice two or three times a week, and that fit nicely with my high-school schedule.

We furnished our own uniforms—or, in most cases, partial uniforms. No one had a complete outfit. I had pants and a beat-up helmet, and I usually wore sneakers.

Often only nine or 10 guys showed up for a game. Then we drafted bystanders and instructed them to "just crouch in the line and don't do anything." Our schedule included games with other Y's and a snooty private school nearby that looked upon us merely as cannon fodder. Usually our games were attended by a roaring crowd of about 10 people.

This was long before separate offensive and defensive teams. Everybody tackled and blocked. I was one of the quarterbacks. I had never been a football hero, but in my last season, we beat the snooty school team with a "Hail Mary" pass from me to a teammate in the last few seconds.

My football career was finally a success. Whenever my receiver and I met in the years that followed, that memorable play always came up in the conversation. We enjoyed basking in the memory of when we had been young, tireless, full of life. There should be a law against aging.

I went to a college where football was big business. The players were all high-school stars on football scholarships, so trying out never entered my mind.

However, we dormitory guys occasionally went out back and enjoyed a game of touch football, which was fairly close to the variety we'd played back in the park.

I'm strictly a spectator of both professional and college football nowadays. However, whenever I see a successful Hail Mary, my fantasy mode kicks in. Once again, that's me out there at quarterback, poised for the game-winning toss! My receiver buddy died years ago, but I bring him back to life for our moment of fame. I can still see him standing behind the goal line, surrounded by would-be tacklers, grinning as he holds up the ball.

So much for my football career. It was no big deal, but it was fun. Still is, especially on Monday nights. ❖

Jesse's Teammate

By Jack Friedberg

I was sort of a teammate of Jesse Owens on the track team at East Technical High School in Cleveland, Ohio. Why do I say "sort of"? Well, Jesse was the star of the team. He led the team to the national track meet, where we won the national championship. Jesse scored more points all by himself in that national meet than did the entire second-place team.

I, on the other hand, was the fourth-best miler on that team. And since schools were only permitted three entries in each event, I could only run in those special relays where they had a two-mile relay for four half-milers and a four-mile relay of four mile runners.

Jesse graduated before I did. He went on to Ohio State University and national recognition.

I graduated in June 1935. The following summer, since I was in good physical condition and enjoyed distance running, I decided to enter a 10-mile race in one of Cleveland's suburbs.

By the time that race took place in late summer 1936, Jesse had made international headlines in the 1936 Olympics. He was asked to run an exhibition sprint on the day of the race, and, ever obliging, he agreed to do so.

There were only 14 of us entered in that 10-mile race; back in 1936, only a few of us "nuts" participated in long-distance runs. I wound up in second place and was awarded a loving cup. Afterward, I showered and dressed and, proudly carrying my second-place trophy, went over to watch my former teammate run his exhibition.

He was warming up as I approached. When he saw me carrying my cup, he called out, "Hey, East Tech, how did you do in that grind?"

Jesse Owens remembered me! He stopped his warm-up long enough to take my cup in his hand, look it over and enthusiastically compliment me on it. By this time, I was walking on air. Jesse was talking to me and complimenting me in front of all those people who had turned out to watch him.

I will never forget how gracious he was to me that day. ❖

My Game

By Patricia J. North

"Score! Score!" the spectators shouted. During a pause in the action, the referee consulted the scorer's table, stepped to the center of the court and blew his whistle. He loudly announced the tally at this stage of the game. The game was basketball. The setting was an outdoor dirt court on the high-school grounds in a small rural town. I witnessed the scene often during my high-school years in the early 1940s when I played on the girls' team.

We had no scoreboard. Our lights were four large outdoor bulbs strung on wires above the court. On windy evenings, the lights swung back and forth, distorting our vision. In dry weather, dust flew, even though the court was leveled and packed down to a hard surface. Obviously, wet weather meant no games. In northwestern Missouri we never knew what to expect from the weather.

All the small-town high schools in our county conference had similar courts, except for two of our rivals. When we lost to those teams, we complained jealously that they had more opportunity for practice in their indoor gyms. When we won, we declared that we were tougher from enduring outdoor practices.

We had no scoreboard. Our lights were four large outdoor bulbs, strung on wire above the court. On windy evenings, the lights swung back and forth, distorting our vision.

Since our high schools did not have the capacity for football, we began basketball practice and games in early fall. As the season progressed and nights turned colder, loyal spectators bundled up and stamped their feet to keep warm as they sat on the wooden bleachers. A small, enthusiastic cheering squad encouraged us.

I started as a freshman on the first team since most of the previous year's players had graduated.

Our coach had difficulty assembling girls for a new team. He had coached at one of our rival schools and told us he would be happy if we'd just beat them.

We did—but it was our only win that year.

Our girls' team played a three-division game in which the court was marked off in thirds, with a jumping center and a running center in the middle third. At the initial toss-up, each jumping center tried to knock the ball to her running center who then tried to pass to her forwards against the opponents who were trying to gain possession. Working the ball through three sections of court did not contribute to a speedy game.

The town team match was an annual event. The town team was a group of former high-school players including whoever was available to play any given year.

One player on the team had been my grade-school teacher. She was a tall, athletic woman who could heave a pass the length of the court, over the heads of the centers.

That was her way of moving the game along. Most fascinating, however, were the black, knee-length bloomers she wore—the uniform of her playing days years before.

At our first conference game, we were dismayed to learn that the conference was now playing two-division ball. I never knew why our coach didn't get word of the change; apparently the method had been discussed at conference meetings, because he knew that he now had to place three guards and three forwards in each half of the court.

"What's going on? How do we do this?" we asked, confused. Centers had to take different positions and try to adapt. We all had to learn a new kind of play then and there. Somehow we stumbled through it.

It did make a better game, and after we became accustomed to the rules, we liked it. We played two-division ball the rest of our high-school years.

In my sophomore year, a new high-school principal was hired. She felt that our home-made basketball uniforms were not appropriate. Our school colors were red and white, and we wore dark red corduroy shorts and white T-shirts with sewn-on numbers and lettering. Not all the uniforms had been cut from the same pattern, however, and some had been handed down from previous players.

Our principal's idea of a "proper" uniform was a one-piece cotton gym suit, and she ordered one for each of us. But they were not available in our school colors, so we were suited in light green. *Green?* What a disappointment not to wear our school colors! In those days, we did not consider protesting; still, I was embarrassed about playing in those suits that I felt were too old-fashioned and the wrong color.

In November we competed in the county tournament, held in the gym at a business college in the county seat. When our team entered the large gymnasium—it was the first conference tournament for most of us—we were awestruck.

My heart sank as I heard the echoes of bouncing balls and shrill whistles, and I looked up at an immense crowd of spectators. This was a new world! We had no opportunity to practice on the floor, but our panic subsided as soon as our game began. From then on, we just played ball.

In subsequent seasons, the tournament setting became less intimidating. Certainly it caused us no difficulty my sophomore year, when our team, the conference champs, also won the tournament. It was doubly thrilling because our boys' team won their championship the same year.

In a small memory book assembled by some of our students, a snapshot of our winning team was included. There we were, 10 of us, lined up in our green gym suits *a lá* the Radio City Music Hall Rockettes. Someone had labeled the photo "Ten Tempests." Maybe it was indicative of the tempestuous approach we adopted to overcome our poor showing my freshman year. We had become real players in just one year.

In retrospect, the setting, the conditions and the type of play I so vividly recall all seem rather primitive. But it was no less exciting at the time. Now, as a spectator, I enjoy watching a women's game that has evolved into fast, full-court play. Basketball was my game years ago, and it's still my game. ❖

Canada Corners Softball

By Charley Sampsell

In the spring of the year, the young men's fancies at Canada Corners School turned to thoughts of softball. I was an eighth-grader with aspirations of becoming our starting pitcher. As the cold Michigan winds of March gave way to the warm showers of April, we shed our high-tops and donned our new tennis shoes to become mercurial in fleetness of foot. When the spring thaw mud had evaporated, bats, balls and fielders' gloves appeared, and every recess and noon hour was consumed with their use.

Since Canada Corners' enrollment only averaged around two dozen students, no intersquad rivalry was possible. We were hard-pressed to field a nine-player team without reaching below about the fourth grade. Competent girl players were as welcome as males.

Our daily games were always "work-up." Three batters were chosen to start. As the first batter was put out, the catcher would replace him, the pitcher would become the new catcher, the first baseman would become pitcher, etc.

Bats, balls and gloves appeared, and every recess was consumed with their use.

By mid-April, this spring training revealed the competence—or lack thereof—of each player, and the teacher was able to select a dozen or so players for a team. We were usually able to play games against Parkville, Angevine, Hall and Strong schools before the school year ended in May.

On the afternoons games were scheduled at other schools, Teacher would load our equipment in his car. Then the team of nine to a dozen players would pile into the seats and trunk or onto the running boards for the slow, three- or four-mile trip over rough gravel roads to the opposing school. Sometimes, one of the car-owning parents would assist with transportation, thus easing the customary overloading. Through good fortune and a high degree of care by the drivers, no one was seriously injured during our game-day travels.

In 1938, our big game of the season promised to be against Parkville. This was a one-room elementary school like our own, but it was located in a one-store, one-gas-station village. Thus we considered their players to be "townies" and felt obliged to prove the superior ballplaying abilities of "country boys."

Two of my Sunday school classmates at West Mendon Evangelical Church, Ralph and Marlon, were players on the Parkville team.

Facing page: *Safe At Base* by Alan Foster © 1927 SEPS: Licensed by Curtis Publishing

Alan
Foster

I knew that the losers would be the butt of lots of razzing during the summer to follow.

Teacher decided on a Tuesday in late April that we were as ready as we were going to get for the big contest. He called my best pal, Len, and me to his desk after lunch hour, gave Len the keys to his car, and told us to take his challenging note to the Parkville teacher and arrange for the game at their school on Friday.

In 1938 at Canada Corners, it was not unusual for unlicensed, 13-year-old boys to drive the country roads of the neighborhood. We all began our driver's training sitting on our fathers' laps as soon as we were large enough to grasp and turn the steering wheel. When we could reach the accelerator and brake pedals, we were considered fully competent.

Len and I fired up Teacher's Model A with Len at the wheel and jackrabbit-started out of the schoolyard. As we jetted toward the 8-foot-wide drive onto the gravel road, Len was surprised by the sensitivity of the Model A's steering compared to his folks' Model T. His intended 90-degree turn to the left became a 120, and we slapped into the 2-foot-deep ditch just west of the drive with jarring impact.

Canada Corners School, 1938. I'm standing on a wire fence, wearing my high-tops.

We quickly ascertained that our slight miscalculation had not been observed, backed up and proceed in a more orderly manner. The rest of our journey was uneventful, and the Friday contest was confirmed.

When the big game started, we were proud to field our best team. Len, Dick, Walt, Cerny, Irwin, Vernie, Don, Paul and I moved from one position to another with each passing inning, showing impressive versatility. The score seesawed up and down, with Canada Corners setting the pace, only to be overtaken by Parkville.

Finally the last inning arrived. We—the good-guy visitors—posted a one-run lead in the top of the frame. Excitement mounted, at least for those of us about to take the field for the last three outs. When Teacher handed me the ball and said, "Close it out, Chuck," my pulse rate doubled and I began to sweat as though it were late August instead of a cool April afternoon.

My first few pitches were a disaster. I walked the first batter, gave a single to the next and began to panic. Then the third hitter popped up to the first baseman, the next grounded out to third, and only one player stood between us and the big win. The next batter was my church classmate and archrival, Marlon. We both knew that a whole summer's bragging rights were hanging on the next at-bat.

Suddenly everything snapped into sharp focus. The panic was gone. The sweating stopped, and it was a game we had played dozens of times before. I gave him a ball. He took a mighty strike. I gave him two more balls, one low and wide, clear to the backstop, and another over his head. I burned in a hot one, right down the middle. He took a weak swing.

Full count. Not much left: One strike, one out, one game, one season for the two of us. I took my most impressive windup, full arm swing, and lobbed a rainbow ball right down the middle. Marlon wasn't fooled. He timed it perfectly, and put all his muscle into the power arc of his big bat.

But Somebody smiled down on me. The ball hit the bat about 4 inches above his hands and returned straight to me on the second bounce. I underhanded it to first for the easy third out—and the right to remind my pal about the big game for the rest of the summer.

The rest of our games for my final season in organized ball were strictly a mixed bag. I pitched some, played a lot of second base, scored my share of runs by devious means rather than power hitting, and had more fun than I deserved. But nothing topped that last inning in the 1938 Canada Corners-Parkville game. ❖

Country School Picnic

By Dorothy Behringer

When our country school was over for the year we always had a big picnic day. We really planned that day. We decided a week or more in advance who should bring what to eat. Everyone brought something different.

We had "cleanup day" on the last day of school. We always cleaned everything up, inside and out, so it would be ready next fall when school resumed. The blackboards were wiped clean with a damp cloth, and the floor was swept clean with smelly green sweeping compound. Everything was checked out and straightened up.

When the inside was done, we went outside and tidied the whole school yard, teacher and kids alike. That day she was one of us. Every bit of scrap paper or junk was picked up. We raked with rakes we had brought from home. By the time we were done, all that was left were the stones and green grass.

We never had to have janitors at our school. We kept it clean. When we left school in the spring it was always in order for the fall classes.

Then the picnic day came. Most of the mothers would come. Usually we headed for the coulee (woods). Most times we walked down into the coulee, as it was a short mile or so from the school. We'd find a shady place down under some big trees, spread a blanket or two on the ground, and spread out all the food we'd brought.

Once that was done, kids ran every which way. The best place was the little creek that ran all summer long. All of us had to dip our feet in that. When we tired of wading, we played lots of games, ran lots of races and even played softball.

When noontime came the mothers called and kids showed up from all directions and down from tree branches. It was time to eat. We built a small bonfire and roasted wieners and marshmallows. They tasted so good along with all the other food. We had every kind of food one could want.

Later, someone would drive into town in their Model A Ford and come back with a canvas bag that held cans of ice cream. It stayed good and cold in that canvas bag until we could eat it. We ate ice cream until it was all gone. We very seldom had ice cream at our house, so it was a wonderful treat!

We seldom had ice cream at our house, so it was a wonderful treat!

Other years when we had our picnic, one of the fathers would come to the school with his cattle truck. Most of the food was put into the cab, and we'd all climb into the truck box. Then off we'd go, yelling like crazy.

He would drive us off to someplace farther away than usual, and what a time we had! We would go for miles—food, hollering kids, bugs and all in a stinky cattle truck. We yelled at everything along the way. When we passed another car or person on the road, all of us kids yelled and waved. They must have thought we had "lost it"!

Why, we even yelled at telephone poles, cattle and horses! Can you imagine a truckload of kids yelling and waving at telephone poles and animals in the pastures? Oh, we were noisy!

I can sure remember how I felt that last day of school when I carried my papers and things home. And how good I felt when we all had cleaned up the mess we had made that whole year, inside and outside our school. Everything was left "shipshape"!

Close your eyes and think of your last day of school. See it, feel it, remember it. ❖

Kurt Ard

Prom Knight

By Anita Biase

I wasn't exactly among the most popular young women in Mrs. Pepper's sixth-grade class. You know the popular group: the ones who are always giggling together, wear the latest fashions and the best hairdos, etc. I don't know if they are born beautiful or just are really good at grooming, but they always look great. In my day, they were the ones who wore poodle skirts with huge safety pins. They were the best dancers and were always sneaking smokes in the bathroom because they thought it was wicked and made them look sophisticated.

Anyway, popular I was not. I was short, pimply and fat. To make matters worse, I had no bosom. I don't think too many people were fooled by the toilet paper I stuffed down my front.

He was, and always would be, my prom knight in shining armor!

The teachers liked me because I was smart. Mrs. Pepper even let me pass out invitations for my upcoming birthday party during study hall. This was almost unheard of, but back then, there was little concern about "fairness." If a teacher felt that a student deserved a certain privilege, she could bestow that privilege without worrying about the other students expecting the same. The teacher was the undisputed boss of the classroom.

I was one of six children and we didn't often get to have parties, so I was really excited about this one. I invited everyone in my class so as not to hurt anyone's feelings. Besides, I figured that not everyone would be able to come and if I invited all of them, at least I would have a few guests—and a few gifts! We were going to have hot dogs and root-beer floats, and I had halfway persuaded my mom to stay in the back bedroom while we played Post Office and Spin the Bottle. I wasn't really interested in boys yet,

Facing page: *First Prom Dress* by Kurt Ard © 1959 SEPS: Licensed by Curtis Publishing

but there was just a hint of things to come in my dreams at night.

Besides, I knew that all the popular kids liked those games, and I wanted to be "in." It was just possible that this party would be my debut into the crowd of young people I'd always envied on one hand—and disdained on the other.

Well, the big night arrived and I was really nervous. I was wearing a new full skirt over three crinolines, and my brother had loaned me some of his new hit records. My hair had been fixed by a neighbor's daughter, who had teased it up really high and attached a tiny bow to the front, right above my bangs. She said I looked "real cute."

When he tried to hold my hand, his palms were all sweaty and oily.

The doorbell rang, and my little sister let in a boy named Dale Holcombe. Dale sat three rows over from me in study hall and was very shy. I didn't know him very well, but I tried to make small talk to make him feel comfortable. We had a lot in common; if I was the least popular female in class, Dale was easily my closest male counterpart. He sported ears that looked like jug handles, a large, crooked nose and thick glasses. The parts of his body never seemed to quite go together. I didn't know anyone who would be caught dead with Dale Holcombe!

To make a long story short, no one else showed up. That's right, we sat there watching the food go cold and the soda pop go flat for about an hour before my father decided to rescue us. He cleared his throat a few times and mumbled something about how "We must have put the wrong date on the other invitations." Then he thrust some money at Dale and suggested that we walk to the nearby Dairy King to get a soda or a chocolate milkshake. I was already humiliated, and now my father was railroading the homeliest boy in school into taking me on a pity date. I was too humiliated to even cry. Neither one of us knew how to turn down the offer graciously, I guess.

Dale tried to be nice, but when he tried to hold my hand, his palms were all sweaty and oily. *Yuck!* We had decided to go to the local movie theater instead, to see the new King Kong movie. I guess Dale felt sorry for me and wanted to try to salvage the evening for me somehow.

His parents picked us up after the movie and when we got to my house, Dale walked me to the door and said goodnight, just like we had been on a real date. I tried to be polite, but it was pretty hard. I said goodnight quickly and ran upstairs. At the time I thought it was the worst night of my life. I hoped that I wasn't going to have to be friends with him now. The other kids all made fun of him, and, well, it was hard enough being me already.

Over the next few years, time began to work its wondrous miracles and, for most of us, the scales began to drop off the toads. By my junior year in high school, I had slimmed down and filled out in the right places and had learned how to camouflage my pimples. I soon starting having Saturday-night dates and even went steady for a while with a passably cute guy named Jimmy Clark.

I was vaguely aware that Dale Holcombe had changed from a frog to a prince with considerable aplomb. Indeed, all of his body parts seemed to move together all at once. He grew 6 inches taller and became captain of the football team. Girls buzzed around him like bees.

I was painfully aware of how little good this amazing metamorphosis was going to do me. I had, after all, treated this budding Adonis rather cruelly. He had phoned several times after the night of my sixth-grade catastrophe. I always managed to have my long-suffering mother answer the phone if I thought it might be him.

I would stand near the refrigerator and mouth the words "I'm not home!" I knew my mom hated fibbing for me, but I was her daughter, so she did it.

I guess he finally gave up on me. The calls stopped, and he hadn't even looked at me in the past three years. I could hardly blame him. I had been pretty cold. Why would he want to look at me anyway? He had all of those cheerleaders at his beck and call! He certainly hadn't been deprived of female company since his braces came off and his knees straightened out, now had he? So, there it was. Dale went on with his life, and I went on with mine.

This all came back to me on the night of the senior prom. I was in my bedroom crying all over my new pink tulle dress from Hartson's Emporium. My date had taken sick with mononucleosis the day before, and in all the confusion, none of his family had thought to call me until I was already dressed.

This "kissing disease" was supposedly a romantic illness, but all it meant to me was the most important night of my whole school career had been ruined!

I had to suffer through the offers of my father and brother. Each was willing to be my escort, if begrudgingly. Their kind offers were declined. It would have made a heartwarming scene in a movie, but in real life, it would've only been embarrassing. I was doomed.

Then the doorbell rang. I opened the door and there was Dale. He looked a little uncomfortable standing under the yellow porch light, as if he thought I might yell at him or kick him off my porch or something. He was wearing a gray tuxedo, cradling a bunch of carnations in one hand and fiddling self-consciously with his tie with the other. It seemed that some misfortune had befallen his date, and he was also without a partner. I'm sure he had a lengthy explanation, but I didn't hear it. All I heard was his stammered invitation. Since his date couldn't go and he'd heard that mine was sick, he'd just thought that I might like to go with him!

They say opportunity knocks just once, but I was lucky enough to get a second chance. Dad's wink at Dale was barely perceptible as I turned to let Dale help me with my coat.

It wasn't really important what circumstances led Dale to my door again. I realized that he was, and always would be, my prom knight in shining armor! ❖

Graduating Fashions

By Carolyn Mott Ford

I recently attended the graduations of my youngest niece from high school and my granddaughter from the eighth grade. They, along with all their classmates, male and female, wore caps and gowns. As I proudly watched them receive their diplomas, I couldn't help but think back over the years. How I wish we could have worn caps and gowns when I was a young graduate!

When I graduated from high school, we were allowed to wear white gowns similar to those we wore to proms in the 1950s.

My parents took me shopping, and I picked out my dream dress: white tulle with an insert of white daisies decorating the strapless top. There was a puff of a white tulle stole, as well.

My 17-year-old mind decided that nothing would look better with that gorgeous dress than a glamorous tan.

I am pictured in my gown.

So off to the beach I went with my friends. I got a tan, but it was hardly glamorous.

On graduation night, my shoulders and arms were bubbling. The sunburn was just about to start peeling as I stepped up to receive my diploma. Perhaps I should say I "stumbled up," because I was unaccustomed to wearing high heels. The shoes were extremely high, with pointed toes.

How much easier life would have been if I could have hidden under a cap and gown! I wouldn't have had to toil over that eighth-grade dress, nor would I have had to worry about a tan to set off that white gown.

At the very least, I could have hidden my overdone shoulders. And maybe the cap and gown could have covered a pair of low-heeled shoes so that I could have graduated not with fashion, but with a bit of dignity! ❖

Broomcorn Romance

By Joan Clayton

"They are turning out school tomorrow to pull broomcorn? You've got to be kidding!" I threw my books down on the couch in a huff. Mother gave me a stern look, and her soft voice answered: "They are short of hands because of the fall harvest, and if the broomcorn isn't pulled, the farmers will be losing their living. It's just for a day, and they need all the help they can get."

My mother's compassion for others had always touched my heart—but *pulling broomcorn?* Broomcorn was the main crop around our little New Mexico town in the 1940s. It had to be pulled at just the right time, or the farmers wouldn't get a good price for it.

"I don't even know how to pull broomcorn," I protested. "Besides, high-school kids shouldn't have to do that for nothing. The least the farmers could do is pay us for it."

"They don't have the money," my mother replied. "You are only thinking of yourself. Think of how blessed we are, and God will bless you in return. What you do for someone else returns to you."

"I don't even know how to pull broomcorn," I protested.

I learned a lesson in selflessness and humility that day, a lesson for which I would always be thankful.

Early the next morning—and I mean *early,* like daybreak—my friends and I met at the high school. Our self-esteem plummeted. We thought it beneath our dignity for "Sweet Seventeens" to be reduced to such menial tasks.

The farmers divided us into groups, and we rode to the fields in the backs of pickups. Soon we arrived. I gazed and gasped. The tall stalks of broomcorn, waving burnished golden heads, looked like the bastions of fortified walls just waiting to be challenged.

"Keep up your row or you'll get behind," Farmer Zeke said. "I'll help you. I want to thank you for giving me a day of your schoolin'."

Yeah, right, I thought.

"You make little racks like this, " he explained to us sleepy teens. "Bend over two stalks and make a little bridge. Then you lean the broomcorn you've picked upon the two stalks. That makes it easier for me to come by in my truck and pick them up later."

Bless Farmer Zeke, I thought. *What a hard way to make a living.* I decided right then and there to have greater appreciation for brooms.

The chaff from the broomcorn scattered all over me as I touched a stalk. I had to bend it over just to reach the broomcorn at the top.

Pulling the broomcorn out of the stalk brought another challenge. I discovered that if I didn't do it with just the right slant, the stalk of broomcorn wouldn't even come out, and the huge, sharp blades of the green, shiny leaves would cut my hands.

That's when I lost all pride and put on the big, ugly cotton gloves my mother had sent with me. I had already given up by wearing tacky overalls and my dad's oversized shirt. The straw hat she also made me wear smashed my hairdo, and the sweat running down my head and face itched like crazy.

"Great day for pulling broomcorn," Zeke called. "There's plenty of water at the end of the row. I don't want my pullers getting thirsty."

It had to be the hottest day of the year—no clouds in the sky, just heat steaming down without a breeze. Gnats flew all over the place. Add to that the scratching from a field of giant broomcorn stalks with sticky tumbleweeds here and there, and you had one miserable gal.

"Having a hard time?" I looked up to see who had stepped into my row and was now pulling my row of broomcorn. Wow! It was Emmitt Clayton, the most handsome boy in school. All the girls had a crush on him. Now, here stood the prize catch—and he was helping *me.*

"It's hard to pull broomcorn if you're not very tall." He already had pulled an armload and was fixing a rack for it before I could say anything. *Hey, letting school out for broomcorn pulling wasn't such a bad idea,* I thought. *Never mind the itching and scratching, especially when this tall, dark and handsome hunk is standing right next to me!*

At the lunch break we talked and laughed and even exchanged sandwiches. My mind raced. *This broomcorn pulling has turned out to be fun*, I told myself.

By late afternoon, the field had become a sea of golden stems of perfect broomcorn on little piles of racks. Farmer Zeke would have a good winter. He drove us home, and I thought I saw a tear in his eye when he thanked us again.

As for me, I will confess to falling behind a little on purpose with my row. Many years later I married that tall, dark and handsome guy and we've been happy ever since. Brooms now have special memories for me. They remind me of someone who swept me off my feet.

Whenever I pass a field of broomcorn, I throw a kiss, for had it not been for broomcorn and Farmer Zeke, I might not have married the man of my dreams. Like my mother said, "What you do for someone else returns to you." ❖

Two Johnnies

By Larry Nestor

It was right after World War I. My dad was a student at Sacred Heart Catholic School in St. Louis, Mo. He was named John and was called "Johnny," and his best friend was Johnny Spath. Each was a good student, and so the sister teaching them often had them do odd chores around the school—especially putting up the chairs after a gathering in the auditorium/gymnasium. She knew that in spite of the interruption to their studies, they would have their homework in on time.

My dad and his friend loved to play basketball. When Sister sent them upstairs to the gym to put away chairs, they could not resist the chance to shoot a few baskets. They would hurriedly put the chairs away, leaving them a few precious minutes to practice shooting foul shots.

But there was one little problem: The basket was right over their classroom. Sister had a sharp ear, and she would know that they were not going about the business of putting chairs away if she heard the ball bounce on the floor just above her. So one Johnny would shoot while the other stood under the hoop and caught the ball before it hit the floor.

My dad told me that for the most part, their plan worked. Occasionally, however, a rebound would get away and bounce sharply. I can just picture the two of them scrambling to get the ball before it bounced a second time. One bounce might be mistaken for a misstep, or a chair leg dropping to the floor. But two or three bounces? Their first thought was to get ahold of it before it made any more noise. Then they would freeze in position, hardly even breathing.

Once in a while, Sister sent someone upstairs to see what was going on, and sometimes she headed upstairs herself. Fortunately, a heavy door opened onto the second floor, and when they heard that door slam, the two Johnnies would hastily hide the basketball in a nearby locker, wipe the perspiration from their faces, and be removing the dust from their fingertips just as the student or Sister entered the gym.

Phew! That was a close one! ❖

Is It Soup Yet?

By Edna Krause

A new idea came to our K-12 school in 1938, and it was all because of our teacher, Mr. Gucky. He stood before the Harris, Mich., student body and asked, "How many of you would like a bowl of hot soup everyday at school?" My taste buds sprang into action as I glanced about the room. Hands popped up like mushrooms in a meadow after a warm spring rain. As often as we had soup at home, hot soup in school was something new, and we were all excited about it. We clapped and cheered.

Grinning from ear to ear, Mr. Gucky just stood there for a moment and allowed the racket to explode. Finally he motioned for us to quiet down. "We have many obstacles to this bold idea," he said, "and I can't promise how long hot soup can be provided."

Indeed, he had many problems to overcome. There was not a single corner in any room of the school to set up a kitchen. And while he was sure that parents in our farming community would gladly donate vegetables, he was not so sure who would do the cooking. He knew that our overworked mothers, many of whom had small children, were unavailable. And depending on older students might create difficulties.

"How about you, Gen? I hear you know your way around the kitchen."

But unknown to Mr. Gucky, there was one born-to-cook senior sitting before his very eyes: my sister, Gen. She came from a home where her many brothers and sisters begged their mother to "Let Gen cook." They openly admitted that Gen made better meals than their mother did. Gen's cooking skills were honed from years of practice, and her cooking ego was blown sky-high from the many compliments her siblings gave her.

When Gen heard the buzz that Mr. Gucky was looking for someone to do the school cooking, she threw her shoulders back and walked around the halls with a glow on her face. Soups were her specialty, and she told her best friend, Viola, that she'd rather cook than study any day. Still, she was a tad shy about walking up to Mr. Gucky and volunteering.

I had a strong interest in who should cook soup in school. And, as a freshman, I took Spanish from Mr. Gucky. So after class, I walked past his desk and said, "Gen makes the best soups in the world."

A few days later, Mr. Gucky walked into our 9–12 room and brought us up to date on what was going on with our hot-soup program. He told us the Harris Grocery Store had offered to donate soup bones some days. And there would be a charge of 2 cents a bowl so that we could afford to add meat to the pot occasionally. He informed us the soup program was beginning the following week. "Do I hear any volunteers to do the cooking?" he asked, peering at the senior girls. (At that time, no male would do "woman's work," as cooking was called.)

Not one hand went up. After a long pause, Mr. Gucky asked, "How about you, Gen? I hear you know your way around the kitchen."

My sister, Gen, at the time of the story.

I held my breath. From my desk by the window, I glued my eyes on Gen. At last she flashed her white-as-snow smile and said, "Sure, Viola and I can do it."

Later that same day, a classmate leaned toward my desk and whispered, "Your dad is here." We inched closer to the window and watched my dad unload a wagonful of vegetables as Prince and Nellie stood swishing their tails. Papa carried burlap sackfuls of potatoes, carrots, rutabagas and cabbage into the school basement. How proud I was of Papa!

By the end of the week, vegetables waited in the school basement. A cooking spot was set up in a book closet off Mr. Gucky's room, where a two-burner propane gas plate and a few other essentials were installed. Above the gas plate, four 2-quart glass jars of home-canned tomatoes glowed red on a shelf. To the right of the shelf, a bag of dried onions hung from a nail.

The day arrived. Gen and Viola were ready. Gen brought her well-planned timetable from home. When necessary, the girls strutted proudly from classroom to cooking station.

After history class, their creative work continued. Into the huge pot went water, soup bone, salt, pepper and a large, sliced, dried onion. Viola pulled the red rubber band that sealed the cap on the 2-quart jar and poured the whole tomatoes into a bowl. After dicing the tomatoes, she emptied the bowl into the pot.

When the first whiff of home cooking wafted by our noses, we students looked at each other and smiled. Years before the Campbell Soup television ad flashed on home TV screens, classmates asked Gen and Viola, "Is it soup yet?"

Gen studied the timetable again. An hour had passed since the first ingredients began to bubble. It was time to add chopped carrots and rutabagas. The girls kept one eye on the clock during English literature class, knowing that chopped cabbage and potatoes had to be dumped into the pot in half an hour. Gen's smile never left her face as she saw admiring glances from all directions.

Before Gen turned off the burner, she performed her secret ritual: She tasted the soup and added salt and pepper. Then she poked the largest chunks of vegetables. Satisfied, she turned off the soup to allow it to cool.

At 12 noon, the pot of soup was carried to a table in Mr. Gucky's room. Bowls brought from home were lined up next to the pot, and Gen and Viola stood ready to fill the bowls of bright-eyed students as they waited in line.

There was a partylike atmosphere as students enjoyed their first bowl of school soup. Mr. Gucky walked from room to room to see how his idea was being received. By the look on his face, it seemed that what he heard and saw pleased him greatly.

From time to time, other girls took turns making the soup. In fact, the volunteer sheet was always full. The hot-soup program continued for the rest of the year, and it was still going strong when I graduated three years later. ❖

Because of "Soap"

By Charles C. Walther

In the 1940s, I was attending Foreman High School on Chicago's North Side, which had an enrollment of several hundred dedicated scholars. Each student was assigned to a homeroom with a homeroom teacher. We met with our homeroom teacher several times a week and were given information concerning activities and special events.

One of the classes at the school was journalism. That class published a newspaper called *The Foreman News*. The paper listed club data, special events and the achievements of students who deserved special recognition. The homeroom and homeroom teacher of the student who was featured were always listed. Students boasted whenever they or their homeroom was recognized in this way.

Unfortunately, the room and class to which I was assigned was seldom mentioned; no one in our room excelled in athletics or served on special groups or organizations. My homeroom classmates and I were devastated.

One day I wrote a poem. When I showed it to Patty, the young lady who sat in front of me, she suggested that I submit it to the paper. But I was a bashful young lad, so I refused. I did not want my name associated with a poem.

Still, there was the possibility that some recognition would be accorded our room if the poem was accepted and published. And so for this reason, I typed it in typing class and signed it "the Unknown Author of Miss Stern's room 323." Then I inserted it in the journalism submission box when no one was looking.

Several days later, a representative from the paper came to our homeroom and asked who the "unknown author" was. I sat quietly, ignoring him. When no one answered, the student asked again, but still there was no response.

Then the representative stated that he would read the poem and perhaps that would cause someone to remember. He then read:

Soap

I'll give a salute to Lincoln,
Washington, Tyler and also Polk.
But I'll never cheer the face of
The guy who invented soap.

I wonder if the cavemen,
After sliding down a dirty slope,
Would stick their hands in water
And lather them up with soap?

Do the monks up in the mountains
In a lonely hut of tin
Take soap into their shower
And rub the lather in?

Do the little boys in Sweden,
When there's soap inside their eye,
Yell, "Help! Oh, gosh, Mamma!"
And then begin to cry?

And what about the Arab,
Or the far-off Congo man?
Would he eat his bar of soap
Or rub it on his pan?

Soap is sure a menace;
It's something we all fear
When Mother takes us by the neck
And says, "You forgot the other ear."

The paper representative again asked, "Who wrote the poem?" I sat quietly. But Patty shouted, "I know who did it, I know who did it! Charles did it!"

Well, the poem was published with my name, and our homeroom and teacher gained recognition. Thereafter, I wrote several more poems that were published in the *News* with my name affixed. Soon I was called "the Poet Laureate of Foreman High." And all that occured just because my classmate Patty told on me. ❖

The Road to Reading

By Linda R. Cook

It was December 1955, and I was a happy second-grader at our little country school in northern California. This was my second year under the tutelage of Mrs. Leila Brent. She was a warm and loving teacher who made me feel special and valued. During my first year with her, she opened up the world of books and reading for me. I devoured *Dick and Jane* and *See Spot Run.* I learned quickly and practiced my phonics everywhere I went.

During second grade, Mrs. Brent also introduced me to the thrill of competition and prizes. A reading contest was in progress involving colorful cutout cars climbing a mountain road, up and over the top and down the other side to the finish line. For each book a student read, the car would jump a car length ahead.

I was green-eyed-monster jealous of Nellie, and I wanted to trounce her.

I was bumper-to-bumper with Nellie, another voracious reader. I was green-eyed-monster jealous of Nellie, and I wanted to trounce her at every opportunity. She was the spoiled daughter of a well-to-do rancher, and to my way of thinking, she had everything.

Nellie had no idea what hand-me-downs were; she always wore perfect dresses and shiny patent leather shoes. This was my chance to outshine her, and I was determined that my car would be first over the mountain. I would win that special prize waiting at the end of the road.

December proved to be a hazardous with high winds and torrential downpours. Mudslides had already closed some local roads. Rivers and creeks were rising, and extensive flooding created havoc with incoming town traffic.

Mrs. Brent had promised that there would be a Christmas party at the end of the week, and the winner of the Road to Reading contest would be announced. In addition, the entire school—about 100 students in grades one through eight—would receive a special gift. But this would only happen if the roads stayed open.

I woke early on Party Day to blasts of thunder and flashes of lightning. Rain pounded our home, and the wind howled. I was terrified that school would be closed. I stayed glued to the kitchen window, desperate for a glimpse of the bus. The minutes continued to tick away. It seemed like a miracle when I spotted it.

At school, by 11 a.m., students were gathered in the gymnasium in preparation for the contest awards and the Christmas party. Stomach churning, knees wobbly and fingers crossed, I stood at the front of the line with Nellie squeezed in against me. She was, of course, dressed in red velveteen and glossy red patent slippers, her hair styled in perfect curls.

Mrs. Brent quieted the students, gave thanks for the hold in the weather, and proceeded to announce the name of the contest winner. Nellie had to poke me as my name was called. Dazed, I stumbled to the podium and accepted first prize, hardback editions of *Black Beauty* and *Cinderella*. I'm sure I smiled graciously at Nellie as I floated from the stage.

But the greatest gift was yet to come. Our school was one of the first to receive the services of the county traveling library. Students eagerly filed outdoors, oblivious to the weather, to see the mud-spattered Bookmobile. As the contest winner, I was honored to be the first to cross its threshold. A bibliophile was born.

Forty-eight hours later, the county suffered the worst storm damage in its history. Roads and bridges washed away, homes flooded and food and emergency services were flown in by helicopter. But my Road to Reading car had weathered the storm. Battered and crinkled, I parked my car in the winner's slot, safe and secure, at the end of the road. ❖

New York to Washington

By Barbara Cole Feiden

Dinner in the dining car. That's what I remember best about my first train trip in 1940. I was 14 years old, and I was traveling from New York City to Washington, D.C., as one of four proud but nervous representatives of my school's Junior Red Cross chapter.

About halfway through our four-hour trip (our coach-seat ticket was $5.57!), a cheerful, uniformed Pullman porter came through our car. He jangled his bell and paused when he came to our seats. "Time to eat, young ladies," he said and smiled broadly.

We headed to the dining car where we were bowed into our plush seats. As I remember it, there were large white napkins, good china, an alarming number of pieces of silverware, and a menu full of choices. We had chicken soup, and memory tells me that when the train went around the curves, all three of us managed to spill quite a bit. I don't remember much of what we ate, but I know that we finished off a tasty meal with chocolate ice cream, chocolate syrup, chocolate fudge and chocolate sprinkles. Then the gracious porter escorted us back to our seats.

When we arrived at Washington's imposing Union Station, we got lost among the enormous arches, sculptures and pavilions while we waited to be met by our guide/chaperone. We took a taxicab (an adventure in itself for young teens in those days) and oohed and aahed as we drove past the White House, the Capitol, the Washington Monument and the Lincoln Memorial.

"How do you ever get used to seeing all these wonderful buildings?" I asked the cab driver, somewhat naively.

He replied, "Just like you get used to seeing the sights of New York." (I let him think I lived right in the Big Apple and had seen everything there was to see. I certainly didn't admit to coming from Yonkers, a pleasant but uninspired suburb of New York.)

Two very busy days in Washington followed. My memories of the official meetings, the lectures, the speeches and the exhibits have faded with the years, but my recollections of the trip to the Arlington National Cemetery, the lawn party and the farewell banquet are still clear. Most vivid in my mind is meeting—well, almost meeting—first lady Eleanor Roosevelt.

All of us jabbering young Junior Red Cross delegates from the then-48 states stood vaguely at attention. Mrs. Roosevelt walked up and down between the lines, smiling, exchanging a word or two and shaking hands, first to the left, then to the right. Unfortunately, I was to her right when she reached out to her left, but I did get a smile from her, a moment I've remembered happily all these years.

And then, all too soon, it was time to head back to the train, back to New York and then home by subway and trolley car to Yonkers.

I wrote an article for the local newspaper and for my Hawthorne Junior High School paper, the Chanticleer. I quoted Oliver Evans, one of the early inventors of a steam-powered vehicle, who, in 1800, wrote, "The time will come when people will travel in stages, moved by steam engines from one city to another, almost as fast as birds can fly, 15 or 20 miles an hour. A carriage will start from Washington in the morning, the passenger will breakfast in Baltimore, dine in Philadelphia and sup in New York the same day."

No breakfast or supper was served on the Washington–to–New York train in 1940, but I did eat a good lunch in the dining car as we traveled through Philadelphia. I've forgotten some of the panel discussions I wrote about in my letter to the Yonkers paper, but I certainly remember spilling my soup for the second time, and enjoying the delicious chocolate ice cream, chocolate syrup, chocolate fudge and chocolate sprinkles. ❖

Senior Class Trip

By Katherine Pulliam Nelson & Carol Carlson Smith as told to Dan Nelson

In June 1946, it seemed like freedom had finally returned. Gone were the worries, rules and rationings of World War II. We were 18 years old and graduating from Varna (Ill.) High School. Our class decided to take a trip to Colorado—quite an undertaking since many of us had never been more than a few miles from Varna. We had worked hard selling magazine subscriptions to finance the trip.

When the big day arrived, 10 anxious graduates (three boys and seven girls) and two uneasy chaperones piled into two cars along with all our luggage. The guys were chaperoned by Principal Peterson, who doubled as our math teacher. He was strict but fair, and had only one rule for us girls: "No primping in the morning. Those who know you know you can do better, and those that don't know you don't care."

Mrs. Trulin, the girls' chaperone, was also our Latin teacher. She was quiet and businesslike, expecting us to act in a proper manner.

The time passed quickly as we traveled the two-lane roads. At night we stayed in mom-and-pop motels or pitched our tents under the stars. We visited some astonishing sites while we were out West: Royal Gorge in Colorado, the Corn Palace and Mount Rushmore in South Dakota, and, of course, the Wall Drug Store.

At the Royal Gorge, we drove our cars over the abyss on a rickety wooden bridge. It was scary but exhilarating, too. Some of the braver students traveled to the bottom of the gorge on the small train that scaled its sheer walls.

At the Corn Palace, we were surprised to find that corn could be used to make murals. In Illinois, all we did with corn was eat it!

The pride we felt as Americans standing in front of Mount Rushmore in South Dakota was indescribable. Patriotism was running high after our victory over the Axis powers.

What can you say about Wall Drug in Wall, S.D.? After reading their advertising signs for hundreds of miles, how could we *not* stop?

Our trip lasted only 10 days. Money was beginning to run low, and we girls began to miss our boyfriends. When we arrived home, some of the mothers hosted a banquet in our honor. It was a great opportunity to tell our stories and relive our experiences.

It was an amazing summer. None of us who took that class trip during that unbelievable summer of 1946 will ever forget it. ❖

Below: Our group on Royal Gorge Bridge, June 1946.

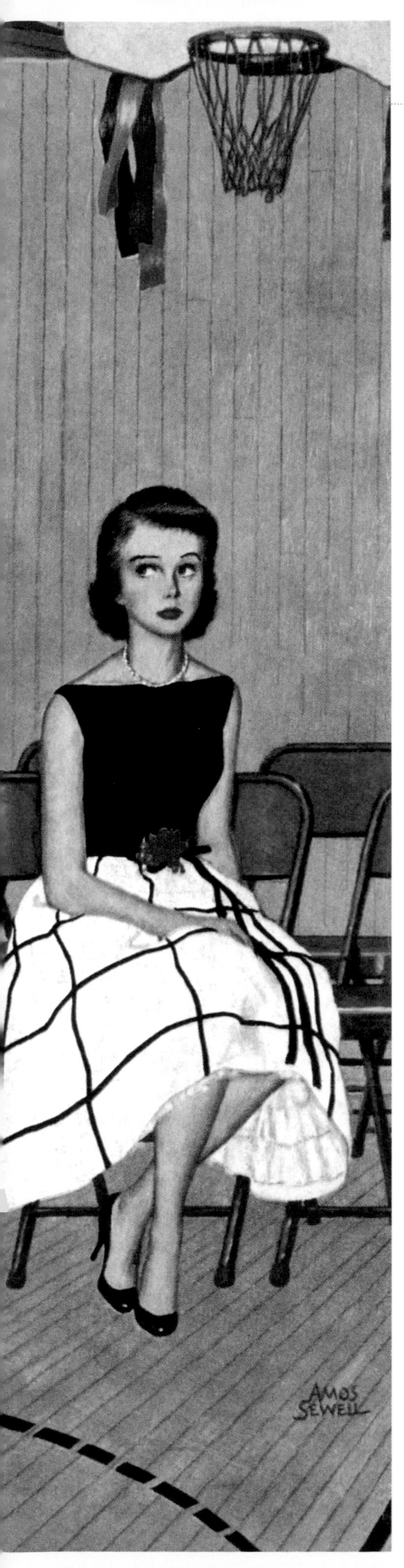

Best of All

By Phyllis Smith Brewster

It was the best of all times to have been in high school in 1939–1943, and the best of all possible places, Bexley, Ohio. There and then was all the innocence, freedom and fun of uncomplicated youth. There was peace in the country, at first, and there were the Big Bands. In September 1939, dressed in our back-to-school skirts and oversized sweaters, we went off with anticipation and a little unease to begin our freshman year.

I may have been more nervous than most, for I was in conflict with my mother about sweaters and saddle shoes. Most of my classmates wore cashmere sweaters and Spaulding saddle shoes. My mother knitted my sweaters and resisted making them as big as the style was, and took me to Gilberts to buy saddle shoes that cost $2, instead of Spauldings that cost $6.

Formals at the end of school were held at a country club or a hotel.

Bexley had three elementary schools but only one junior high, so by the time we got to high school—about 500 of us—we almost all knew each other, many of us since kindergarten. The teachers knew our names, our parents knew each other, and everyone knew my dad. He was Coach Smith, and the chemistry teacher. In some ways, this notoriety was an advantage to me, but in at least one instance it was not. When I was rushed to an invitational club, I learned that I had been "blackballed" by a senior who had gotten an "F" in chemistry from my father. Fortunately, I didn't learn about this until after she had been pressured to withdraw her "no" vote, and I had received the coveted invitation to join.

The "swinging years" music defined our social life. The rhythms, the lyrics, the dancing—Artie Shaw, Harry James, Jimmy Dorsey,

Facing page: *Who Will He Ask* by Amos Sewell

Tommy Dorsey, Glen Miller, Stan Kenton, Sammy Kaye, Cab Calloway! In Columbus, we heard them all in person at the Valley Dale. We filled the huge, barn-size pavillion, jitterbugging to the fast pieces and swaying romantically to the slow, sentimental music. Between Big Band appearences, we bought 78-rpm records of everything they played and memorized the words that captured the mood and romance of the time—sweet, simple, uncomplicated, naive.

On Friday nights there were football or basketball games or dances in the gym, each sponsored by a school club like Girl Reserves or Hi-Y, and almost always featuring a local live band. Girls had to have a date; boys could go stag. Popularity was measured by how many cut-ins you got from the stag line.

Formals during Christmas holidays and at the end of school were held at a country club or a hotel. We girls wore long dresses and the boys, tuxedos.

There were hayrides, roller-skating parties, weiner roasts, sorority spreads and movies—movies, movies, movies! No weekend was complete without at least one. The theaters in downtown Columbus—the Palace and the Ohio—were special treats. The Ohio had the edge because, after the main feature, Roger Garret and his organ rose from the orchestra pit, filling the theater with music. On the screen, a little bouncing ball showed what word to sing at what moment.

After the movies, we went to Swenson's Drive-in for hamburgers and car-to-car visiting, or to the Circle (a round park) where we also did car-checks to see who was with whom. Couples who stayed in their cars and "necked"—the period word for hugging and kissing—were considered "jerks"—also a period word.

Was it all fun? Of course not. My biggest worry was being popular, which I never was. The yardstick for measuring such status ranged from girls who had two or three invitations to a dance to those of us who usually got to the dance but were asked late and not by a popular boy. Standard measurements for popular boys were looks, clothes and a smooth line. Neither character nor brains was considered an item.

Our "crowd," as we called ourselves, numbered about 15 girls. Fortunately for those of us without a date on a Friday or Saturday night, there was always someone with whom we could go to a movie. We never, however, went to a theater where we might be seen by the popular girls and their dates.

On occasional weekends, parents let their daughters have what we called "a brawl," a misleading term, as there was never any misbehavior—no alcoholic beverages, and the parents were always in residence. It was simply a gathering of our classmates, playing cards, dancing, drinking Cokes and fooling around.

Some weekends one of the girls would have a slumber party. Fifteen or 20 of us would stay up most of the night talking and laughing before we finally fell asleep four or five to a bed, or on blankets on the floor.

To school, we wore those saddle shoes or penny loafers, baggy sweaters and wool skirts. On Saturdays, blue jeans and men's oversized shirts were the dress code. Guys had crew cuts, girls pompadours. If you were going steady with an athelete, you wore his gold football or basketball on a chain around your neck.

During study hall, we passed notes to our friends and scarcely ever studied. Between classes we met our boyfriends at our lockers. Lunch in the cafeteria could be had for 25 cents, but most of us went home for the 90-minute lunch hour. Although smoking was forbidden everywhere, most of us tried it. Very few of us enjoyed it.

After school, if you didn't have detention (a 45-minute punishment) or band practice or play rehearsal or tennis team or Latin Club, if you weren't on the yearbook staff or the school paper, you walked with your friends to Wentz's pharmacy for a vanilla Coke and a lot of interaction.

The raspy voice of Superintendent Claude Dietrich came over the homeroom loudspeaker: "May I have your attention, please." He seldom got it.

Our unforgettable faculty numbered 24, with one administrator, Principal Russell Kessler. Journalism teacher Ruth Geist prepared her students for successful careers in that field; John Schacht illustrated geometry with his three-dimensional figures that he later patented and sold. Berniece Mullins postured in drama classes and in directing the senior play. Miss Bethel instructed no-nonsense typing and shorthand; Ira Ferbrush taught algebra, Mr. Tipton taught history, Miss Selbach taught English, and Miss McCurdy, cooking and sewing. All of the women were "misses"; married women were not allowed to teach.

Very few Bexley high school students had cars of their own, and those who did sported old jalopies they had fixed up to chug around town. Some fortunate few were able to borrow the family car on special occasions, like dates, but mostly we walked. Nobody but *nobody* would be caught riding a bicycle.

In December 1941, three months into our junior year, Pearl Harbor was bombed. Although the world around us turned upside down, the war had very little effect on the rest of our time in high school. The lyrics of the Big Band music now focused on the painful separations of lovers: *I'll Never Smile Again*, *Don't Sit Under the Apple Tree*, *I'll Walk Alone*. Our high-school bandmaster joined the Navy, and our P.E. teacher joined the WAVEs. But those departures were not important in our lives, and the songs of parting didn't ring of reality for us yet. None of the boys in our class was old enough to volunteer or be drafted.

Two war-related assemblies did stir deep feelings. One, during our freshman year, featured our classmate Max Bruck, who had recently come from Germany, his Jewish family having escaped Hitler's death net. From the stage in our auditorium, he told us about having to wear the Star of David on his sleeve; he told us how no Gentile would speak to a Jew; how little kids would throw stones at him as he rode his bike to school. Many of the residents of Bexley were Jewish and we all had Jewish friends. It was chilling!

The other program was in 1942, while Kenny McClure, a graduate of the class of 1941 and brother of our classmate Bruce McClure, was home on leave from the Army Air Corps. He shook our complacency when he told us about his buddy who had been flying next to him in formation over the Pacific. When his friend's plane suddenly burst into flames, Kenny watched in horror as the plane started to nose down, and his friend gave him a farewell salute. I still get a lump in my throat when I think about it.

In October of our senior year, we sponsored a war stamp drive, and in November, a scrap drive. In January we gathered books and magazines for the armed services. In the spring of 1943, a Red Cross project raised $100 from the high-school students. In the spring, tests were given to the senior boys for the Navy V-5 and V-12 programs. My boyfriend enlisted in the regular Navy. Our yearbook was dedicated "to freedom" and to the 200 former Bexley students who were then serving in the Armed Forces.

But that spring of our senior year was a culmination of everything good—warm weather, spring sports, love in bloom. The National Honor Society elections were announced in assembly. The senior play, *George Washington Slept Here*, kept the cast after school for weeks. I was there every afternoon (except when the girls tennis team had a match), even though I only had one line: "Tennis, anyone?" But I still got nervous when it was my time to walk onstage.

And so our high-school years came to a close—a blend of the innocence and blythe spirit of the late 1930s, foreshadowed by the clouds of war of the early 1940s. It was the end of one era and the beginning of another, though we didn't know it then. Now we remember it as a time of great freedom—from responsibility, from hard work and from loss and pain. Those years from September 1939 to June 1943 were a life all to itself—our high-school life, and the best of all times. ❖

The Close of School

Submitted by Dorothy Jean Schroeder

This poem, "The Close of School" is from the end-of-school souvenir program for the Forest Glade school, Snohomish County, Wash., dated 1906. Emeline Bergeron taught grades one through eight in the little one-room schoolhouse. She had 21 students that year in five grade levels. The program belonged to my father, Edward M. Gemmer. It was found among his most treasured possessions when he died in 1982 at age 90. ❖

The time has come to say farewell
For now our term is through;
To sound our present school days' knell
And bid you all adieu.

"Farewell"—a word that stirs our hearts,
That moves our feelings strong,
That sadness frequently imparts,
And makes us linger long.

For months together we have met
And conned our lessons o'er,
And done our best to know and get
A part of Learning's store.

Thro' all the days I've labored hard,
And often during night;
Your progress was my sole regard,
Your welfare my delight.

And oh! my pupils, I have tried
To do the best I could;
I've ope'd the book of knowledge wide,
And hope you've understood.

Get wisdom, said the Sage of old,
Who spake in sayings wise;
More precious she than gems or gold,
Or any other prize.

And richer far than greatest king,
Or treasures of the mind,
Are they who drink from out her spring,
Or worship at her shrine.

With all your getting therefore get
An education true;
'Twill be a crown with jewels set,
A pow'r to each of you.

And thanks for all your favors shown,
For cheer, which toil beguiles;
For roses in my pathway strewn,
For all your love and smiles.

And at the parting of the ways,
We at this moment stand,
And soon we'll close our dear school days,
And take each other's hand.

Most fondly do I wish you well,
And hope you each may be
An ornament where e're you dwell,
And from all vices free.

And now the swift, descending sun,
Proclaims the time is here;
So goodbye each and ev'ry one,
Farewell, my pupils, dear.